Hindu Prayers, Gods and Festivals

Hindu Prayers, Gods and Festivals

Tumuluru Kamal Kumar

Transliteration by
Dr. Swarna Sambasiva Rao,
Retired Professor of Sanskrit

PARTRIDGE

To order additional copies of this book, contact
Partridge India
000 800 919 0634 (Call Free)
+91 000 80091 90634 (Outside India)
orders.india@partridgepublishing.com

www.partridgepublishing.com/india

Contents

This book has the blessings of

His Holiness Jagadguru

SRI SIDDHESWARANANDA BHARATISWAMY

Siddheswari Peetadhipati – Courtallam,

Thirunelveli district,

Tamil Nadu

Introduction

Many Indians have felt that Hindu children living abroad have not fully developed their cultural moorings. To some extent this is also true of children living in the metros in India. It is with this in mind that I thought I should compile a book for children to read and get an idea about our culture.

This book is only a compilation of prayers, Gods and festivals known to thousands in India and found in several books. The prayers have been written in English for the children, particularly those who are overseas and may find it difficult to read in Sanskrit or Hindi or any other language. An attempt has been made to provide explanations for easy understanding. There are several hundreds of prayers but I have restricted these to a few so that the book can be concise. The parents can help the child to pronounce the words.

I have also covered about the symbolism of our Gods. I have deliberately not covered the stories and puranas relating to the background of a certain symbol. For example Shiva has the Ganga flowing through his matted hair. While I have covered only the symbolism of what it means, I have not endeavoured to cover the story and the reason for this.

Hindus see God as the ultimate energy in and all creation but not as identical with it. Man finds it easier to associate himself with an image rather than words or an abstract concept. Divine symbols provide insight into the essence of the reality they represent. The divine image for a Hindu is the visible expression of the deity. Symbols and idols help as a link between the finite and the infinite.

All the different forms are different aspects of the one God or Paramatma. The trinity are the three different aspects of one supreme God. Universal Truth is one but not exclusive and hence just as in human relationships there is a diversity. The divine in Hinduism is conceived in a variety of forms, manifestations and avatars, so that a devotee can choose a form that suits his liking and aptitude. Lord Krishna says in the Bhagavad Gita "Whatever form a devotee chooses to worship, I instil the faith of that devotee in that very form."

Originally Hinduism was known as Sanatana Dharma or Eternal Religion and this recognized that divinity had both male and female attributes.

The Vedas are known to be Apauruseya or of impersonal origin. They are eternal and all gods are aspects of the same one Supreme Spirit, God, Creator, Divine Father or Mother whatever we may like to call him.

We often speak of Brahman (God) and the universe as two different aspects though inseparable; Brahman as the permanent and enduring aspect and universe as the power of Brahman. Gods are depicted with various hands indicating infinite capability.

Prayers, symbolism and the festival related to a God are covered in a sequential manner.

This book is not meant to be a treatise but an introduction to Prayers, Gods and Festivals. There have been varied interpretations in various books or by various Swamis about Gods and festivals. I have covered only to the more common ones.

This book is intended to promote educational and cultural values.

***

First Published: 2015

Back cover picture is of Adi Shankaracharya, the proponent of the Advaita philosophy and the one who first established the Swami (monastic) order.

The pictures in this book have been obtained under copyright from Mr. T. Mahesh (the original painter of the pictures) of IDEA FACTORY, Panjagutta, Hyderabad – 500034, India. The author is not responsible for copyright violation, if any. These images are being used only for educational and cultural purposes.

Some General Tips for Prayer and Japa

Sit in the same place every day.

Sit in a comfortable position.

Face East or North.

Sit on a rug or a woollen cloth.

Start with a sloka on Ganesha and then your Guru.

A japa mala aids in concentration.

Mental japa is very powerful.

The times that are effective for prayer or japa are dawn, dusk and mid day.

Have faith in the sloka, mantra – it increases its effectiveness.

Chanting of mantras generates positive divine vibrations.

Japa or prayer must be done with Bhava (feeling) and preferably with the knowledge of the meaning of the prayer.

Ganesha

Prayers to Ganesha

Shuklaambaradharam Vishnum
Shashivarnam Chaturbhujam
Prasanna Vadanam Dhyaayeth
Sarva Vighnopa Shaantaye

Salutations to Lord Ganesha, the one dressed in white, who has the colour of the moon, who has four arms, is pleasant faced and who protects us from all obstacles, on him I meditate.

Vakrathunda Mahaakaaya
Suryakoti Samaprabha
Nirvighnam Kuru Me Deva
Sarva Kaaryeshu Sarvadaa

O Lord with a curved trunk and large body, your lustre is like that of ten million suns, Please remove all obstacles that come in my way.

Ekadantam Mahaakaayam
Lambodara Gajaananam
Vighna Naashakaram Devam
He Rambham Prana Maamyaham

I bow down to the Lord with one tusk and a large body and stomach with the face of an elephant, who removes all the obstacles and who is also known as Herambh or beloved of the Mother.

Ekadantam Mahaakaayam Taptakaanchana
Sannibham
Lambodaram Vishaalaaksham Vandeham
Gananaayakam

I bow down to the Lord of all, who has one tusk, has a large body, whose complexion is like that of molten gold and who has a big belly and very large eyes.

Gajavaktram Surashreshtam Karna Chaamara
Bhooshitam
Paashankushadharam Devam Vandeham
Gananaayakam

I bow to the God who is the leader of Shiva's ghosts, who has the face of an elephant, who is supreme among all the deities, whose ears are large and who is armed with a noose and an axe.

Mahaa Ganesha Pancharatnam

Mudhaa karaastha modhakam
sadhaa vimukthi saadhakam
Kalaadharaava thamsakam
vilasiloka rakshakam
Anaayakaika naayakam
vinaasithebha dhaithyakam
Nathaa subhaa sunaasakam
namaami tham vinaayakam

Ganesha is the one with a pleasant face who holds the sweet 'modak' in his hand, wears the crescent moon on his head. He liberates us from misery and provides direction to those who are lost. He removes the obstacles for those who pray to him. My salutations are to Him!

Nathetharaathi bheekaram
navodhithaarka bhaaswaram
namathsuraari nirjaram
nathaadhikaapa dhuddharam
sureshvaram nidheeshvaram
gajeshwaram ganeshwaram
maheshwaram thamaashraye
paraathparam nirantharam

Ganesha, with the glow of the rising sun, is the commander of Shiva's army. He eliminates the devotess suffering. I take refuge in Ganesha.

Samasthaloka sankaram
nirastha dhythyakunjaram
dharetharodharam varam
varebha vakthramaksharam
krupaakaram kshamaakaram
sudhaakaram yasaskaram
manaskaram namaskruthaam
namaskaromi bhaaskaram

Ganesha gives peace to the entire world. He is infinite and immutable. He is forgiving. He brings happiness, success and purity of mind. My salutations are to the luminous Ganesha.

Akinchanaarthi maarjanam
chiranthanokthi bhaajanam
Puraaripoorva nandhanam
suraarigarva charvanam
Prapanchanaasa bheeshanam
dhananjayaadhi bhooshanam
Kapoladhaana vaaranam
bhaje puraanavaaranam

Ganesha, the merciful, who removes the suffering of those who have no other refuge, destroys the demonic forces and negative tendencies in us. He dissolves the delusions of this illusory world. I pray to Him, the one venerated in the ancient Vedas!

Nithaanthakaantha danthakaanthi
manthakaantha kaathmajam
Achintyaroopa manthaheena
mantharaaya krunthanam
Hrudanthare nirantharam
vasanthameva yoginaam
Thameka danthameva tham
vichinthayaami santhatham

Ganesha, the one with the broken tusk, the son of Lord Shiva, he is the formless absolute (his form is beyond the grasp of the intellect), he is infinite, he is the Remover of Obstacles, he lives in the hearts of yogis forever and ever. I reflect solely upon Ganesha, forever and ever.

Mahaaganesha pancharathna
maadharena yonvaham

Prajalpathi prabhaathake
hrudi smaran ganeshwaram
Arogathaam adoshathaam
susahitheem suputhrathaam
Samaahithaayu rashtabhoothi
mabyupaithi sochiraath

He who recites this Maha Ganesha Pancharatnam every morning with devotion, these five gems about Lord Ganapati and who remembers in his heart the great Ganesha, will soon be endowed with a healthy life free of all blemishes, will attain learning, noble sons, a long life that is calm and pleasant and will be endowed with spiritual and material prosperity.

About Ganesha

Ganesha is the first son of Shiva and Parvati. He has four hands, carries an axe and a noose, sweets, and keeps his right leg on top of the left one. He has an elephant head and one of his tusks is broken. He rides a mouse. His dress is red and yellow and he has a large stomach.

He is known as Vigneshwara or Vignaraja i.e. the remover of obstacles. He is usually worshipped at the beginning of all ceremonies. He is also known as Ganapati (the head of Ganas), Vinayaka (knowledgeable), Gajaanana and Gajavadana meaning elephant faced etc. He is also known as Pranava Swarupa.

Elephant head – symbolizes wisdom, sharp and discerning intellect. The Elephant head and a human body indicates spirit and nature integrated in an individual i.e the inseparability of the macrocosm and microcosm.

The large ears symbolize great capacity to hear intelligently and absorb ideas. He continuously wrote the Mahabharata when Veda Vyasa was dictating it to him simultaneously understanding the meaning and thus derived wisdom. Wisdom is attained through sravana (listening), manana (thinking) and nidhi dhyasana (recapitulating).

The trunk – It represents enormous dexterity. It can uproot a huge tree, lift a log and also pick up a very small item from the ground. It represents the capacity to stand the ups and downs of daily life (external) and also explore the Self (internal, subtle) aspects and to be able to perform both activities simultaneously. The bent trunk is in the form of Om, the primordial sound known as Pranava.

One of his two tusks is broken – One denotes wisdom (perfection) and the other emotion (manifest imperfect world). Wisdom needs to be used to overcome emotions. It also means to transcend duality – beyond opposites. One tusk was broken during a battle with Parasurama. He used the other tusk to write the Mahabharata as dictated to him by Vyasa.

Eyes – The elephants eyes they say possess an ability to see things bigger than they actually are. It means that one should be humble and see others bigger than oneself.

Four arms – represent omnipresence and omnipotence. They also represent the mind, intellect, ego and consciousness – the things we use to perceive, recall from memory, discriminate and act.

One hand holds pasa (noose) and the other the ankusa (goad). The other two hands are held in Varada and Abhaya mudras.

Axe in one hand – to detach oneself from the world and overcome emotions. He cuts off the devotees attachments and propels them and mankind to an eternal path. The Ankusa (goad) represents anger (krodha) which hurts us. To remain in the world without being lost in it or being adversely affected by it, one should surrender our weaknesses to him. The noose and goad symbolise obstacles to improper behaviour and unrighteous acts.

Sweets (Modak) in one hand – Willing to offer health, wealth and prosperity to his devotees. If we please him he bestows happiness on us and rewards of spiritual seeking. Also means that we should discover the sweetness of the Atman. The realisation of the inner self is very sweet.

Right foot over the left one – In the brain there are two hemispheres. The right side is controlled by the left brain and represents wisdom to overcome emotions (left side controlled by the right brain).

Mouse (Mushika) – One must control ego for the Self to shine and for knowledge and wisdom to dawn. A Mouse represents desires. Also represents the fear and anxiety in man. Ganesha sits on a mouse, his vehicle. It implies that one should control his desires. Mus means to steal. A mouse enters things and destroys them internally. Egoism destroys us internally.

Noose in one hand – stands for attachment that binds. It is Vasuki that served as a rope in the Kshirasagara Mathana – to realize the divine nectar.

The pasa and ankusa represent attachment and anger which make us unhappy.

The snake belt that runs round his waist represents energy in all forms.

Red and yellow dress – Red symbolizes activity and yellow symbolizes peace and divine love. Ganesha performs all his duties in perfect peace, love and harmony.

The large stomach – capacity to face pleasant and difficult situations and experiences. He is the one who removes all obstacles (Sankataharana). It also indicates that all the worlds are within him.

The fourth hand is in a blessing pose – he blesses the entire humanity.

Gana means category, group, clan. Pati means Lord. He is the Lord of all categories in creation. Isha means Lord and hence Ganesha means Lord of all beings. Anana means face and hence Gajanana means elephant faced.

Ga – Gati or final goal. Ja – Janma or birth. Gaja means the lord from whom the worlds have emerged and to whom they will eventually go to or merge into.

Ganesha is sometimes represented by 5 heads, 10 hands and 3 eyes and riding a lion. He holds lotus, pomegranate, battle axe, kamandala, lute, broken tusk, sugarcane (inner layers are very sweet), ears of paddy, bows and arrows, thunderbolt, rosary and a book.

Ganesha Purana, Mudgala Purana and Ganapatyatharvasirsha Upanishad are devoted to the glorification of Ganesha and his worship. Ganapathi gained Buddhi, Riddhi and Siddhi by winning the race and circumambulating the parents (Pradakshina) which is considered as equal to going round the world. His spouses here represent success and prosperity. He is worshipped in various forms such as Vijaya Ganapathi, Herambha Ganapathi, Sankataharana Ganapathi, Trimukha Ganapathi, Urdhva Ganapathi, Lakshmi Ganapathi etc.

The Siddhi Vinayaka Vrat (Vratam in the South) is performed for overcoming obstacles.

Ganesh Chaturthi

Ganesh Chaturthi, a very popular Hindu festival, is Lord Ganesha's birthday which is on shukla chaturthi in the month of Bhadrapada (sometime in August-September). We first worship Lord Ganesha before any other prayers and in ceremonies or before any auspicious work. Ganesha Chaturthi is also known as 'Vinayaka Chaturthi' or 'Vinayaka Chavithi' and is the birthday of Lord Ganesha. It lasts for 10 days, ending on 'Ananta Chaturdashi'. He is the remover of all obstacles and bestower of success in worldly activities. He is the elder brother of Skanda (also known as Kartikeya or Subrahmanya, Karthikeya or Muruga).

Legend has it that Parvati, while bathing, created Ganesha as a pure being from the mud arising from the washing of her body and kept him at the entrance door of the house. He was told not to allow anyone to enter the house while she had gone for a bath. Shiva who was away returned home thirsty. He was stopped by Ganesha. An angry Shiva cut off Ganesha's head assuming Ganesha to be an outsider. When Parvati came to know this she was very upset. In order to console her, Shiva ordered his people to severe and get the head of any living being that is sleeping with its head facing north direction. The devas who went around found only an elephant sleeping in that position. The elephant's head was sacrificed and brought before Shiva. The Lord then put the elephant's head on to Ganesha's body.

Shiva this way made Ganesha worthy of worship at the beginning of any pooja and any major task. He said that worship of Ganesha should be in the bright half of the month of Bhadrapada (fourth day). People should undertake activities only after his worship.

The esoteric meaning is that when we create impurities, we need to remove them and substitute them with Gnana (knowledge) and Karma (action). The elephant is the only being which does both these tasks with its head and tusk.

He removes all obstacles in worldly life and on the path for the devotee thus bestowing success and is therefore known as Vigna Vinayaka. Ganesha represents Om (also known as the Pranava) which is the primordial sound. This is the reason why we invoke Ganesha at the beginning of any ceremony or any undertaking.

Ganesha is also known as Vinayaka, Vighneshwara, Lambodara, Ekadantha, Vignaraja, Gajanana, Gajakarnaka, Heramba, Ganadhyaksha, Phalachandra, Vakratunda, Siddhivinayaka, Surpakarna, Skandapurvaja, Kapila, Dhoomraketu and Sumukha and of course Maha-Ganapathi.

His Mantra is Om Gum Ganapathaye Namah. Om Sri Ganeshaya Namah is also used. Some of the aspirants chant the Ganesha Gayatri Mantra. The Ganapathi upanishad identifies him with the Supreme Self. His legends are mentioned in the Brahma Vivartha Purana.

Ganesha likes modak (balls of rice flour) very much. Legend has it that on one birthday he went round accepting sweet puddings offered to him. The mouse got frightened of the snake and stumbled and Ganesha fell down. The stomach forcibly opened and the modak that he ate came out. Ganesha put them back into the stomach caught the snake and tied it around his stomach. The moon watched this with a good laugh. Ganesha got upset and threw one of his tusks at the moon and stated that on this day no one should look at the moon. If anyone does, it will not be auspicious for him. If anyone looks at the moon by mistake on this day to clear himself from this curse, he would need to listen to the story of Krishna who cleared his character regarding the Syamantaka jewel which is quoted in the Srimad Bhagavatam.

Ganesha and Karthikeya had a disagreement on the issue of being one elder than the other. It was left for Lord Shiva to take final decision. Shiva stated that the one who goes round the whole world and returns first will be judged as the elder. Subramanya went round the world on his peacock. But Ganesha went in worshipfulness around his divine parents. Lord Shiva questioned Ganesha as to how he would be eligible for a prize as he did not complete the task given. Ganesha responded that for him his parents represent the entire universe and I thus have gone round them. Ganesha was then adjudged as the elder of the two brothers. Parvati gave him a fruit as a prize.

On Ganesh Chaturthi day we must meditate on the stories of Ganesha early in the morning. The early hours

17

at around 4 am are the most beneficial. Devotees go to a Ganesha temple and pray with the usual offerings of flowers and coconuts. Devotees should pray with sincere devotion for the removal of all the obstacles in their activities feeling the presence of the Lord in the idol. He can be worshipped at home by the family members or with the assistance of a pundit. One can also pray for inner spiritual strength.

A clay model of Ganesha is made a day before the festival. Idols used at home are small but the ones used for public processions can be tall as high as 10 to 25 feet. It is placed on a pedestal on Ganesh Chaturthi in individual homes or in beautifully decorated tents in colonies for people to come, view and pay their respect. The priests chant mantras to invoke life into the idol. This ritual is called 'pranapratishtha'. Then tributes are paid (shhodashopachara) in 16 ways. Coconut, jaggery, 21 'modakas' (rice flour preparation), 21 grass blades and red flowers are offered with the application of rakta chandan on the idol. Vedic hymns from the Rig Veda and other religious texts apart from Ganesha stotras.

For 10 days, from up to the Ananta Chaturdashi, Ganesha is worshipped. The idol is taken on the 11th day in a festive procession for immersion in a river or the sea. This symbolizes a ritual to see the Lord on his journey back to Mount Kailash while taking away with him the people's miseries. Large processions take place on this day. People chant "Ganapathi Bappa Morya, Purchya Varshi Laukariya" (Ganesha, come again early next year) in Marathi. The festival is very popular in India and particularly in Maharashtra.

Ganesh Chaturthi celebrations were started in Maharashtra by Chatrapati Shivaji Maharaj, the great Maratha ruler with a view to promote culture and patriotism. Ganesha was the family deity of the Peshwas and hence they held similar celebrations.

The freedom fighter Lokmanya Tilak transformed the festival into a major event. He used the festival to help bridge the gap between various castes which helped in community participation and generate a patriotic sentiment in Maharashtra during the days when India was seeking independence from the British. Tilak advised people to set up large idols of Ganesha on grounds and the practise of immersion on the tenth day after Chaturthi. Discourses, folk dances, and musical concerts are also held. It served as a meeting ground for people from all communities at a time when the British discouraged social and political gatherings.

Modak (modakam or vundrallu in South India) is the most important dish made on Ganesh Chaturthi. It is made from rice flour and coconut, jaggery, condiments and sometimes dry fruits as well. A popular sweet dish in Karnataka is karanji very similar to modak in the ingredients and taste.

***

Guru

Vyasa

Prayers to Guru

Gurur Brahma Gurur Vishnuh
Gurur Devo Maheshwaraha
Gurur Saakshaat Parabrahma
Tasmai Shree Gurave Namaha

I bow down to that Guru, who is Brahma, Vishnu and Shiva and who is the supreme Lord himself.

Guru is creator Brahma; Guru is preserver Vishnu; Guru is also the destroyer Siva and he is the source of the Absolute. I offer all my salutations to the Guru.

Twameva Maata Cha Pita Twameva
Twameva Bandhuscha Sakhaa Twameva
Twameva Vidyaa Dravinam Twameva
Twameva Sarvam Mama Deva Deva

You are my mother, you are my father, my relative and you alone are my friend, You alone are my knowledge and my only wealth, You O God of gods are everything to me.

Dhyana Moolam Gurur Murtim
Poojaa Moolam Gurur Paadam
Mantra Moolam Gurur Vaakyam
Moksha Moolam Gurur Kripa

The form of the Guru is the basis of meditation, the feet of the Guru are the basis of worship, the words of the Guru are the basis of the mantra, the grace of the Guru is the basis of liberation.

Om Sahanaavavatu
Sahanau Bhunaktu
Saha Veeryam Kara Vaavahai
Tejasvi Nava Dheetamastu
Maa Vidvisha Vahai
Om Shanti Shanti Shantih

May he protect both of us
May he bless us both with the bliss of knowledge
Let us put our efforts together
May our knowledge be bright and brilliant
May we not hate each other
May peace be within us,
May peace be around us,
May peace be above us.

Brahmanandam Parama Sukhadam
Kevalam Gnaana Murtim
Dwandwaateetam Gaganasadrusham
Tatwam Asyaadi Lakshyam
Ekam Nityam Vimalam Achalam
Sarvadhee Saakshi Bhootam
Bhavaateetam Triguna Rahitam
Sadgurum Tam Namaami

I bow to the Guru, who stands for truth, who gives me happiness, who is non-dual, who is the epitome of knowledge, who is beyond time, who is pure, who is free from likes and dislikes, who is attained by assertions like "Tat Twam Asi" who is one and eternal, who is the witness of the mind, who is beyond this world. I bow to the Guru who is beyond satva, rajas and tamas.

Mannatha Sri Jagannaatha
Madguru Sri Jagadguru
Madaathma Sarva Bhutaatma
Tasmai Sri Gurave Namaha

My Lord, Lord of the creation,
My Master, Master of the universe,
My Soul, soul of all living beings,
To Him, my gloriously radiant Master, I bow down.

About Guru

Guru is a term for "teacher" or "master" in India. The guru-shishya tradition is the tradition of passing on wisdom from teacher to student.

Guru means the imparter of knowledge. It means a person with deep knowledge or spiritual wisdom. According to the Guru Gita, Gu means "beyond the qualities" and Ru means "Devoid of form", meaning that "He who bestows that nature which transcends the qualities is said to be a Guru".

The Bhagavad Gita, is a dialogue between Lord Krishna and his friend Arjuna. The relationship of Krishna and Arjuna is considered as an ideal one of Guru and Shishya. Arjuna accepted Krishna as his guru on the battlefield in Kurukshetra just before the battle began. Krishna also spoke to Arjuna on how important it is to have a Guru – Acquire knowledge from an enlightened master by humility and service. The spirit of self inquiry needs to be developed in the aspirant. The masters pass on spiritual knowledge to the sincere devotees.

A guru is a spiritual guide for his disciples. A true guru has saintly qualities who enlightens his disciples about spiritual and scriptural knowledge. Religious texts such as Manu Smriti regard the guru, mother and father as the ones with best influences on a person. A guru usually lives in an ashram or in a gurukul with his disciples. The lineage of the original guru and his disciples, who carry on the guru's message is known as guru parampara.

A Guru depending on whether the disciple is ready may give diksha (initiation) through his grace to quicken the disciple's awakening. The aspirant receives deep knowledge due to transfer of the guru's consciousness depending on the degree of his attunement and surrender to the master.

Guru Purnima

Hindus give enormous importance to spiritual gurus. Gurus are are considered as a link between the individual (jivatma) and the Immortal (Paramatma). Purnima means full moon day.

Guru Purnima falls in the month of Ashad (July-August). It is a day dedicated to the great sage Vyasa and a symbol of Guru-sishya parampara. Vyasa wrote the 18 Puranas and the Mahabharata. He also wrote the Srimad Bhagavatam and edited the four vedas. Vyasa had taught

Dattatreya who is known as the Guru of Gurus. Vyasa was born on this day and also started writing the Brahma Sutras. This is the day for the disciples to offer their respect to their Satguru. Sage Vyasa is considered as the Adi (original) Guru of the Hindus. Vyasa Poornima is of great significance as the Guru is great importance in Hinduism.

The festival is also celebrated by Buddhists. This was the day on which Lord Buddha gave his first sermon at Sarnath. This day is also known as "Vyasa Purnima".

Krishna-Dwaipayana Vyasa (Veda Vyas) – the author of the Mahabharata – was born on this day and hence it is celebrated as Vyasa Purnima. Veda Vyasa, gathered all the Vedic hymns during his time. He then split them up into four parts based on their requirement in the sacrificial rites, and taught them to his four main disciples. This dividing and editing earned him the honoured title "Vyasa". He divided the Veda into Rig, Yajur, Sama and Atharva. Vyasa means to edit and divide. The Puranas are also referred to as the fifth Veda. Spiritual seekers worship Vyasa and perform a puja of their Guru. It is a good day for the aspirant to intensify his spiritual sadhana. The Guru principle is more active during this day. A disciple's seva done on this day bestows the grace of the Guru for one's spiritual progress.

Hindu monks (sanyasis), observe this day by offering puja to the Guru, during the four months rainy season period (known as Chatur Mas) when they choose seclusion and usually stay at a selected place and have public discourses. The Chaturmas period begins from this day. India has been very careful to keep alive the tradition of Guru-Tattva. There are many devotees who have felt the grace of the Master through various experiences.

This is a day for spiritual seekers to do Guru seva and be open to their gurus to receive divine grace. Saints, Swamis shower people with their blessings and enable them to experience super-consciousness. The worship of the preceptor has been there from times immemorial. In the olden days during Vanaasram period the disciples residing in the Guru's ashram used to learn the scriptures or shastras. If the Guru is not alive, his portrait or picture is worshipped. This is the day to remember Vyasa, the Gurus and the enlightened masters.

This relationship is purely spiritual in nature with no relevance to their ages. It is based on Gyan (Spiritual Knowledge) and Shraddha (Spiritual Practice) as this is of prime importance to the devotee student. The Guru works for the upliftment of his disciples. Upa means near, ni means down and shad means to sit down. Upanishad means sitting down with the Guru to gain knowledge.

In Sanskrit "Gu" means ignorance. "Ru" means the remover of ignorance. Therefore the person who removes our ignorance is a Guru – the only one who removes our ignorance or Maya. Guru is this one who imparts supreme knowledge (Apara Vidya).

Srimad Bhagwatam says "One cannot attain knowledge of Paramatma by performing various rites, penance, renunciation, study of scriptures and worshipping deities such as of water, fire or the sun. It continues by saying that when the dust from the feet of a true Satguru sprinkles on our heads, then one can attain realization of the self."

Serving a Satguru and his ashram greatly help in the process of the development of the disciple. Self realization by one's own efforts is exceedingly difficult. Adi Shankaracharya says: If a person, despite possessing a disease-free body, fame, wealth, and studied the Vedas and scriptures, and even if he wrote many scriptures, but has not surrendered himself to the Guru, then he would have achieved nothing. Our scriptures are unanimous that only a Satguru can release the disciple from bondage.

The Guru is revered as he guides his disciple on the path to self-realization. He also imparts the meanings of the profound knowledge in the scriptures. The Guru is "shrotriya" - the true knower of the real meanings of the scriptures. All the saints of the various schools of thought such as that of Adi Shankara, Ramanuja and Nimbarka have considered the Guru a must to achieve God-realization. Shankaracharya does not encourage disciples to understand the deeper meanings of the scriptures without a Guru.

On Guru Poornima bhajans and cultural performances are organized by ashrams. It is also the coming of the monsoon season which is important for farmers.

Various scriptures and upanishads glorify the role of the Guru. Kabir had said that if God and Guru stand side by side, we should worship the Guru first and then only God as he is the one through whom we can realize God. The Guru's grace dawns if one surrenders himself to his Guru. He also strengthens the faith of the aspirant.

Japa, meditation and study of the scriptures such as the Guru Gita are recommended on this day. It is believed that if one's devotion to God and the Guru is great the knowledge of the scriptures will eventually get revealed. Some ashrams may have continuous Satsang on this day.

People meditate on the form of the Guru and chant the mantra he has given. His feet are worshipped.

It is ideal for an aspirant wake up at Brahmamuhurta (at 4 a.m.) on this day, do japa and meditate on the Guru's feet to obtain his grace. At home one would meditate or worship after mental attunement. Devotees place flowers at his picture flowers, and light a lamp or incense. Many observe moun (silence) which is a good practice. The best worship of the Guru is to live his teachings and do seva to the Guru which would include helping him in his mission.

***

Surya (Sun God)

Prayers to Sun God

Om Mitraaya Namaha

Prostration to Him who is the friend of all and affectionate to all.

Om Ravaye Namaha

Prostration to Him who is praised by all and is the cause for change.

Om Suryaaya Namaha

Prostration to Him who is the guide of all and induces activity.

Om Bhaanave Namaha

Prostration to Him who diffuses light and is the bestower of beauty.

Om Khagaaya Namaha

Prostration to Him who moves in the sky and is the stimulator of the senses.

Om Pushne Namaha

Prostration to Him who is the nourisher of all.

Om Hiranyagarbhaaya Namaha

Prostration to Him who contains everything and is the creator.

Om Marichaye Namaha

Prostration to Him who possesses rays and is the destroyer of disease.

Om Aadityaaya Namaha

Prostration to Him who is the inspirer and the God of the gods.

Om Savitre Namaha

Prostration to Him who produces everything and is the purifier.

Om Arkaaya Namaha

Prostration to Him who is radiant and fit to be worshipped.

Om Bhaskaraaya Namaha

Prostration to Him who is the illuminator and the cause of lustre.

The above are the twelve names of the Sun God for the 12 steps of the Surya Namaskar exercise.

There are many other such mantras on the Sun which have not been given above.

Sankranti

Sankranti refers to the movement of the Sun from one sign of the zodiac to another. There are actually 12 sankrantis in a year. The Sankranti festival which is celebrated refers to Makara Sankaranti – the Sun's transition from Sagittarius to Capricorn in the month of Pushya in mid - January. The festival marks the start of the "northward migration of the sun" or Uttarayana. Makar Sankranti is usually on January 14th/15th.

Sankranti is a solar event; the calendar we adopt is lunar in most parts of India. Makar Sankranti, is a major harvest festival. Sankranti marks the end of the winter season and commencement of the spring season with warm and longer days. Spiritual rituals are usually sanctified in Hindu families during the period beginning from Sankranti.

Makar Sankranti is celebrated with great enthusiasm. This day has been of significance in the ancient epics such as Mahabharat. Hence, it holds a historical and religious significance. It is the festival of Surya (Sun God) who is regarded as the symbol of divinity and wisdom. On this day Surya visits the house of his son Saturn, who is the lord of the Capricorn. It is believed that Sun and Saturn do not get along well with each other. This day therefore symbolizes the importance of the father and son relationship.

Makar Sankranti starts the 'day' of the Gods. Dakshinayana is said to be their night and is the downward movement of the Sun. Auspicious activities are done during this period. As Vishnu eliminated the troublesome asuras by burying their heads under the Mandara Mountain, this represents the beginning of an era of righteous living.

Bhagirath liberated his ancestors who were burnt years ago at the Kapila Muni ashram by doing tarpan with Ganges water on Sankranti. Ganga visited underworld (Patal) for Bhagirath's ancestors to free them from their curse and finally merged into the sea. Gangasagar mela is held on this day at the junction of the Ganga and the Bay of Bengal. Hindus take a dip in the river and perform tarpan for their departed ancestors. People pray to the Lord Sun.

This is the day Bhishma decided to leave his body. Bhishma left his body on Bhishma Ashtami (Magha Shukla Ashtami). He had a special boon of death as per his will (Ichha Mrityu) from his father. Hence, despite lying on a bed of arrows he continued in that position. Hindus believe that the one who dies during Uttarayana goes to heaven.

The festival is known by different names in various parts of India: Makara Sankranti or Sankranti in Andhra Pradesh, Maharashtra, Orissa, Uttar Pradesh, and most parts of India It is known as Uttarayan – Gujarat and Rajasthan, Maghi in Haryana, Himachal Pradesh and Punjab, Pongal (Tamil Nadu), Magh or Bhogali Bihu (Assam), Shishur Saenkraat (Kashmir) and Makara Vilakku (Kerala).

In Gujarat, the celebrations people offer their offerings to the Sun in the form of colourful kites with great enthusiasm, metaphorically trying to reach God. In the rural areas, cock fight events are held. Makara Sankranti is also to honour and worship Goddess Saraswati (the Goddess of Knowledge).

Sankranti is a period of peace and prosperity. On this day, the environment is believed to have more divine consciousness and hence very helpful for spiritual practices.

A holy dip during this period has a special significance. People take a dip in the rivers Ganga, Yamuna, Godavari, Krishna and Cauvery as this is believed to clear one's sins and obtain merit. Apart from bathing in these rivers, worshipping Gods, fasting, performing havan, doing japa and charity are considered as holy deeds. A donation such as gifting of clothes, blankets etc given during the period from Makara Sankranti to Rathsaptami is considered auspicious.

The haldi-kumkum ceremony (turmeric powder and saffron) is used to invoke the vibrations of Shakti which create positive impressions on the mind and increase the devotee's bhakti to God.

The food prepared for this festival is meant to keep the body warm with high energy as it is winter time. Laddus (a sweet) of til (sesame seeds) made usually with gud (jaggery) is a speciality of the festival. In Maharashtra it is called 'Tilgul'. On Sankranti day vermilion and turmeric powder are applied on the earthen pots called sugad and a thread is tied to them. They are filled with carrots, sugarcane pieces, cotton, sesame seeds with jaggery, vermilion, chickpeas and turmeric. Rangoli surrounds five pots each on a wooden seat and they are worshipped. Of the five pots, three are given to married women, one to a tulsi plant and one retained.

Sesame seeds are used during Sankranti for various things including bathing. Eating and distributing tilgul, offering to temple pundits, lighting lamps with sesame oil are all important. Lamps for Lord Shiva and performing ancestral rites (pitrushradh) are done using sesame seeds. Laddoos are made from Til, used for Havan (sacrificial fire) and Tarpan (oblations of water with Til), Til is used as food, and Til is donated in charity. Til is believed to have emanated from Vishnu's body and that the above are ways to wash away our sins. In Maharashtra they say – Til Gul Ghya Ani Gode Gode Bola (Take Til Gul and speak sweetly).

The sun is the source of light and life and the sustainer of our solar system. It is the source of prana and vitality in vegetation. The sun's existence and movements in the cosmos are important. For Hindus, the Sun stands for spiritual light and wisdom. The festival is a reminder to us to try to be away from delusion and begin to enjoy the light within and share with all like the selfless Sun. Sharing with all is the message of Sankranti.

In Andhra Pradesh, Bhogi marks the beginning of Sankranti festival. Sacred bonfire is the main ritual during Bhogi. Kite flying, Rangoli designs also known as kolam, muggulu in Tamil/Telugu. Kanuma, third day during Sankranti festival, is associated with the lifting of Govardhan Giri by Lord Krishna.

There are joyous celebrations in every home. Food and clothes are distributed to servants, farm labour and the poor. The cow, which is considered sacred is worshipped the next day. Birds and animals are also fed. The devotee's consciousness increases due to the celebrations. Love is extended to family members, servants, and animals such as the cow and other living creatures. We learn our oneness of our self with all creation, and generosity.

The consciousness of the devotee expands during the festivals as there is the satisfaction derived by feeding and sharing what one has with the poor and the animals. To obtain love and respect from all is the real wealth of any individual.

The cow is given great importance in our culture

***

Brahma

About Brahma

Lord Brahma is the Creator of the Universe. He is a member of the Trinity of Brahma, Vishnu and Shiva. His consort is Saraswati, the Goddess of learning, the provider of the knowledge required for the process of creation.

He is usually shown as a four faced God seated on a lotus. The four heads also represent the four Vedas, the four directions, and the four yugas.

In the four hands he has a kamandala (water-pot – the waters of creation), a manuscript/book representing religious and secular knowledge, a rosary (symbolizing time) and a lotus flower. The four arms represent the four directions and thus the omnipresence. The four hands also symbolize the mind, intellect, ego and the self, the four aspects of a human being.

The lotus represents supreme reality. The lord sitting on it means he is ever present and rooted in infinite reality. The daily alteration of day and night is credited to Brahma. He is usually shown as arising out of the navel of Lord Vishnu.

He is also seen riding a Hamsa (swan) which is known for its faculty of discrimination. The swan can separate pure milk from a mixture of milk and water indicating ability to discriminate between good and evil. A man of perfection can realize the Supreme amidst pluralities.

He is the uncreated creator and swayambhu. The self existent Lord manifested to remove darkness in the universe. He is cosmically hiranyagarbha, the universal embryo.

His hands are in mudras (Abhaya – protector) and Varada (ready to give boons / fulfil wishes).

The world is believed to exist for one day (one kalpa) for Brahma which is 4.32 billion years of the Hindu calendar and he is believed to sleep for one night after which he restores creation and this process goes on. This process (pralaya) is repeated for 100 years at which stage the universe is dissolved into its constituent elements.

Brih means to grow. He is the creative principle of the universe. His sons were born by the power of his mind. The world undergoes a cyclic process of creation and dissolution in a long process known as the night and day of Brahma. During the day he is absorbed in Brahman waiting for re-creation. At the coming of dawn Brahma springs from a lotus blooming out of Vishnu's navel. The active creator is called hiranyagarbha or the golden egg of creation or the cosmic subtle body. He is said to reside at Brahmapura or Brahmaloka on the summit of Mount Meru.

Brahma created the Prajapathis and the sapta rishis (seven rishis) to help him in creation. He is also referred to as Prajapathi, the lord of progeny. He controls time and causation.

Sometimes he is shown as wearing a deer skin – this represents austerity. And some other times riding a chariot of seven swans representing the seven worlds.

He is not popularly worshipped in India. There are only a few temples dedicated to him. The only temple of Brahma which is well known is at Pushkar in Rajasthan. There are some stories why he is not worshipped.

He does not possess any weapon although sometimes shown with a bow. He created the gods and placed them in the various worlds – for example, Agni and Vayu in the atmosphere and Surya in space.

There is a story about why Brahma of five heads is shown only with four heads.

He is sometimes shown with a white beard which indicates his wisdom. He is called Pitamaha (grandfather) of creation.

***

Saraswati

In Hinduism we also pray to Goddesses. To recognize the feminine is to restore completeness, balance and universality to any aspect. Goddesses represent the active energy of their consort.

Prayers to Saraswati

Saraswati Namastubhyam
Varade Kaamarupini
Vidyaarambham Karishyaami
Siddhirbhavatu Me Sadaa

I bow to you oh Saraswati, the giver of boons and the fulfiller of my wishes, as I start my study with the prayer that I may always be successful with your grace.

Yaa Kundendutushaarahaaradhavalaa
Yaa Shubhravastraanvitaa
Yaa Veenavaradandamanditakaraa
Yaa Shvetapadmaasanaa
Yaa Brahmachyuta Sankara Prabhritibhir
Devaih Sadaa Poojitaa
Saa Maam Paatu Saraswati Bhagawatee
Nissheshajaadyapahaa

May Goddess Saraswati the dispeller of all inertia, whose complexion is white like jasmine blossoms, the moon or snow, who is attired in a spotless white sari, whose hands are adorned with the enchanting veena, who is always worshipped by Brahma, Vishnu, Shiva and other Gods, who is seated on a white lotus, may she protect me.

About Saraswati

Saraswati is the wife of Lord Brahma. She is dressed in white and is shown with a sacred book in one hand and a lotus in another. She plays the veena, a musical instrument. Her vehicle (vahana) is a white swan. She has a peacock looking at her. The meaning is as follows:

Sara means essence and Swa means the Self. Saraswati means the essence of the Self or the flowing one. Like a river she is connected to fertility and purification of knowledge (Vidya) and removal of ignorance (avidya). Saraswati is the Goddess of learning. Saraswati is the shakti or creative force of Lord Brahma. In childhood we are told to pray to Saraswati for education. You will also find the picture of Saraswati in some educational institutions in India. She is the embodiment of education (Vidya), Intellect (Buddhi), Knowledge (Jnana) and Wisdom (Pragnya). She sits on a rock symbolising that knowledge cannot be taken away easily once acquired.

The lotus denotes supreme knowledge – therefore Saraswati personifies such knowledge. The lotus grows in dirty water but blooms outside of it unaffected by it.

Her four arms indicate omnipotence and omnipresence. She holds a veena, rosary, japa mala and a book. Her creative power is all pervasive in all directions. The front two hands symbolize the mind and the intellect.

White saree – white denotes purity; she is the source of pure knowledge. The japa mala (rosary) symbolizes japa and meditation leading to union with the Supreme Spirit or God. True knowledge destroys the ego (represented by the right hand which is holding the mala).

The book represents knowledge and secular sciences. One must first transcend the secular sciences (the book) and then get true knowledge through spiritual sciences (the rosary).

The veena symbolizes that one must attune oneself to the harmony with nature and the worldly life. It also shows the need for cultivation of the finer aspects of life such as arts, music etc. as intellectual greatness without feelings can be dry. The true spiritual devotee needs to work on these aspects as well.

The swan – The swan is said to have a sensitive beak that enables it to distinguish milk from a mixture of milk and water and separate them. The swan therefore represents discrimination (viveka), wisdom i.e. knowledge must be used with discrimination and not with ego (ahankara). The swan is sometimes her vehicle (vahana). The peacock represents behaviour that can be influenced by the external impulses and the environment. One must overcome vacillation or fickleness of the mind. It enables us to focus attention in order to obtain knowledge of the Self. The peacock is glorious, multifaceted and stands for the glory of the mind which can be very attractive and at the same time can impede spiritual growth (avidya). The peacock can therefore symbolize avidya or ignorance.

Saraswati is also referred to as Veenaapaani and Vaagdevi. She is known by the names of Sharada (the giver of essence), Vagiswari (the Goddess of speech) and Brahmi (the consort of Brahma). Vasant Panchami is her birthday.

***

Vishnu

Prayers to Vishnu

Om Namo Narayanaaya

I prostrate to Lord Narayana

**Hari Om
Vanamaali Gadi Sangi Shanki Chakri Cha Nandaki
Sriman Narayano Vishnur Vasudevo Abhirakshatu**

Protect me O Lord Vishnu who wears a garland and who holds a conch and discus.

**Shantaakaaram Bhujagashayanam
Padmanaabham Suresham
Vishwaadhaaram Gaganasadrisham
Megha Varnam Shubhaangam
Lakshmikaantam Kamala Nayanam
Yogi Hrudhyaana Gamyam
Vande Vishnum Bhava Bhayaharam
Sarva Lokaika Naatham**

I pray to the one with a peaceful form, who lies on Adisesha, who has a lotus (of the universe) from his navel, who is the lord of the devas, who has the shape of the whole world, looks like the sky, dark as the clouds, with beautiful hands and legs, who is the husband of Lakshmi, who has eyes that look like the lotus, who can be reached by the yogis in meditation, I bow down to that Vishnu, the Lord of the whole universe who drives fear away, he is lord of all the worlds.

Graaha Graasthe Gajendre Rudathi Sarabhasam
Tharkshya Maaruhya Dhaavan
Vyaaghuman Malyabhusha Vasana Parikaro
Megha Gambhira Ghoshaha
Abibhraano Rathaangam Saram Asimabhayam
Sankha Chaa Pow Sakhe Tow
Hasthaih Kowmo Dakim Apyavathu Harir Asow
Amhasam Samarther Naha

When the great Gajendra, the king of the elephants, was caught by the crocodile in the water, he prayed to the Protector of all the souls and the origin of this universe. It was then only that the protector Lord Sri Hari appeared in front to save him with all his subjects and weapons. Let him protect us from all our sins.

Jale Rakshatu Vaaraaha Sthale Rakshathu Vaamanaha
Atavyaam Naarasimhas Cha Sarvathah Paathu Keshavaha

Let the Divine boar Varaha Avatara protect us from the waters,
Let Lord Vamana protect us on the ground,
Let Lord Narasimha protect us in the forests, and
Let Lord Kesava protect us from all the corners.

About Vishnu

Vish means to pervade. Nu means to enter. One who has entered everything or rather present in everything.

Vishnu means all pervading, one who pervades. He is the preserver who saves one from difficulties, calamities and the protector of all humanity.

He is known as Narayana, one who supports all beings. He represents the maintenance principle of the universe. He is the one who has made the heart of human beings his abode and is the final goal. The goal of all spiritual practice of man is union with Supreme spirit.

Vishnu is usually shown as blue in complexion and his four hands bear the conch, discus, mace and lotus. Blue symbolizes vastness, infinity and represents the space element. Therefore all his incarnations were dark. Blue is the colour of the aura of a divine being who is very active in this world. His consort is Goddess Lakshmi, the Goddess of wealth and his Vehicle or Vahana is the Garuda (eagle), the king of the birds. Sometimes a curl of his hair (Srivatsa) is shown around his neck.

The four arms represent the absolute power over all directions and are symbolic of various powers. The four arms symbolize the four stages of life and the four purposes of life i.e. Dharma (duty), Artha (Prosperity), Kama (Pleasure) and Moksha (Spiritual Liberation). They also represent the four Vedas.

The chakra (discus) is symbolic of the cycle of existence. It comes back to its source after it completes the action for which it is sent out. It represents the wheel of life. The chakra is like the human mind as its thoughts travel very fast. It is called Sudarshana Chakra – It is fearful as it cuts off the heads of the demons. Su means good and Darshan means vision. A weapon to destroy ego. It is a symbol of the mind shining like the sun to dispel ignorance. It is meant to destroy evil and protect the virtuous.

Vishnu is known as Padmanabha – one with a lotus rising from navel. Lotus expresses purity despite being in a muddy lake not affected by the dirt around it. The message is to live in the world but not get entangled into it. It also symbolises detachment. Padma represents the evolving world. When he thinks of creation a lotus springs from his navel along with Brahma who proceeds with the work of creation. The lotus flower is called padma representing the unfoldment of creation and one's realization.

The mace is called Gada in Sanskrit. It denotes the power of time and cosmic intellect. The mace called Kaumodaki represents elemental power and the punishing capacity of the Lord.

The conch (Panchajanya) symbolizes the cosmic sound OM. The conch represents the 5 elements of the universe, the five elements composing the creation, that is, Earth, Water, Fire, Air and Ether.

Vishnu wears a garland known as Vyjayanti symbolic of subtle elements. He wears the jewel Kaustubha around his neck. He also wears another garland of flowers and Tulasi leaves called Vanamala representing the love that binds him to the devotees and their faith.

He is usually dressed in yellow robes – Pitambara – one with yellow garments. He is also shown as sleeping on a mighty serpent (Seshnaag or Anant Nag) floating on water of the ocean of milk Kshirasamudra.

The ocean stands for bliss and consciousness, the serpent for time, desires and maya or illusion. Milk stands for purity and the Lord is on an ocean of bliss. He is the source of creation and expands and contracts at intermittent, regular cosmic periods. Sesha means remainder. Sesha represents the totality of all jivas left over from the previous cycle of creation. Also represents desires – residual desires which need more lives for regeneration until moksha (liberation) is obtained. Ananta means endless. The thousand hoods indicate the innumerable cycles of time. Seshnag represents the sleeping universe. The ocean of milk (our inner subtle body), resides in Kshirasagara (consciousness in man). Vishnu in his dream state represents the time gap when creation stands withdrawn and the universe awaits the birth of a new era.

Vishnu is known as Narayana (Na – Not, Ra – Perishable and Ayana – support i.e. supporter of all imperishable things) and Hari, protector and the remover of sins.

His vehicle Garuda (eagle) represents Veda or knowledge; thoughts travel fast and far. Vishnu sleeping on the snake (desires) and flying the eagle (thoughts) represents control over desires and thoughts.

To ward off perils he incarnates himself from time to time when dharma declines. He assumes a human form only when evil reaches enormous proportions. His principal avatars are ten but some books depict him to have descended in 23 avatars, some called amsavataras or minor avatars to save earth and its beings from destruction. Vishnu was seen in several avatars or incarnations, namely, Matysa (Fish), Kurma (tortoise), Varaha (boar), Narasimha (Lion-man), Vamana (Dwarf), Parashurama (Rama with an axe), Rama, Krishna and Buddha. His last avatar is Kalki which is yet to come. Details of all the avatars are not covered in this book.

He is also worshipped as Venkateswara in Tirupati and as Satyanarayana, the Lord of truth by families for happiness and fulfilment of desires.

His thousand names – the hymn Vishnu Sahasranama has a great effect when chanted with devotion. His abode is known as Vaikuntha (one which does not disintegrate or get destroyed.) The Saligrama is a symbol of Vishnu representing the cycle of creation and the galaxies in motion.

Holi

Holi is a religious festival celebrated by the Hindus in spring. It is a festival of colours on Phalguna Purnima. During the celebration people throw coloured powder and/or coloured water at each other. Bonfires are lit in the evening during the festival, also known as

Holika Dahan. The bonfires are set up in the evenings to celebrate Prahlad's escape from Holika. Holika, the sister of king Hiranyakashipu was a demoness. She was the one who carried young Prahlad to the pyre to burn him. Holika could not survive and got burnt but Prahlad, a great devotee of Vishnu, escaped without any harm. The festival is known as Kama Dahanam in South India. Rangpanchami is on the fifth day of full moon and with that the festivities involving colour end.

In West Bengal and Orissa it is known as Dolyatra or Basanta-Utsav ("spring festival"). In locations connected with Krishna it is celebrated more such as in Braj, Vrindavan, Mathura, his birth place and Nandagaon where he grew up. Holi falls on a full moon day (last one) in the month of Phalgun, signalling the end of the winter season, Purnima usually in March. Holi is also known as Holikotsava, Holika or Dhuli Vandana, Dhulheti, Dhulandi or Dhulendi.

Hiranyakashiapu was the king of the demons. Hiranyakashiapu wanted to kill Vishnu and have the other gods in his control because Vishnu had destroyed his brother to stop him from terrorising the devas. He instructed his soldiers to kill all Vishnu worshippers who enjoyed the protection of the gods. Hiranyakashiapu wanted to be able to have powers equal to Vishnu's so that he could rule over the three worlds. He performed severe penance. The devas destroyed his city during this time as also his palace. The Queen (Hiranyakashiapu's wife) was expecting a child. She was sent by the devas to Narada's hermitage. She lived in his ashram, learnt the scriptures and about the glory of Lord Vishnu there. The child in her womb Prahlad was thus able to imbibe all the knowledge. Narada told the Queen that Vishnu is omnipresent.

Hiranyakashiapu's tapas pleased Lord Brahma. Brahma gave him a boon which made it impossible for anyone to defeat or kill him. Through his boon he sought that he should not be killed during day or night; in the house or outside, neither on earth or sky; not by a man nor an animal; and not by astra nor by a shastra. Such a boon made Hiranyakashiapu very proud. He attacked the heavens and the earth. He asked people not to worship the gods but instead revere him as the all powerful Hiranyakashiapu.

His son Prahlada turned out to be a devotee of Vishnu. Prahlad's teacher ensured that followers of Vishnu do not in any way have any influence on him. When his father asked him what have you learnt? Prahlad said the most important duty to do is to worship Vishnu.

Hiranykashyapu was very angry: "Who taught you such things?" Prahlad remained calm and said Vishnu reveals himself to all who are devoted to him. Hiranyakashiapu got angry and Prahlad was ordered to be killed. The soldiers attacked Prahlad. Prahlad was meditating on Vishnu and hence he could not be touched by their weapons.

Prahlad's teacher tried to get him interested in acquiring wealth and other possessions. Prahlad was not interested in the pursuit of physical pleasures and money. The teacher eventually gave up, when Prahlad told Hiranyakashiapu that Lord Vishnu is omnipresent. Several threats followed but Prahlad continued to pray to Vishnu. An attempt to poison him could not succeed as the poison turned into nectar.

Many efforts were made to kill him. Elephants were sent to trample him. He was a kept in a room with poisonous snakes. Hiranyakashiapu's several attempts to kill Prahlad failed. Prahlad had to finally be made to sit on a pyre on the lap of Holika, Hiranyakashiapu's demoness sister who could not be burnt due to a boon she had. Prahlad kept praying to Vishnu to keep him safe. To everyone's amazement Holika was burnt to death and Prahlad survived unharmed. People celebrate the burning of Holika as Holi.

Hiranyakashyapu questioned Prahlad "Where is your Vishnu? Why is he not in this Pillar? If I don't find him here I will use my sword and behead you. Let Vishnu protect you." As Hiranyakashyapu was just about to strike the pillar with his sword, Vishnu appeared in the form of Narasimha. He took a unique form to be able meet the conditions of the boon granted to Hiranyakashiapu. Narasimha was a half-man and half-lion and killed Hiranyakashiapu at dusk (neither in the day nor in the night), at the entrance on the steps of his house (neither inside nor outside) and killed him on his lap (not in the sky and not on earth) and piercing his claws into Hiranykashiapu (which are neither astra nor shastra).

Holi is also celebrated until Rangpanchmi to celebrate the divine love of Radha for Krishna, particularly in Mathura and Vrindavan. Krishna popularized the festival with his pranks on the gopis. Krishna complained to his mother about his dark complexion unlike Radha's fair complexion. Krishna's mother then applied colour on Radha's face. The celebrations bring in spring season – the season of love.

Another story – Kamadeva (god of love) threw a weapon at Shiva to disturb his meditation. Shiva's third eye gaze was so powerful that Kama's body reduced to ashes. For the sake of his wife Rati, Shiva restored him as a mental image, representing the spiritual state of love rather than mere physical love. The Holi evening bonfire is also celebrated for this event.

The Holi festival also known as Dol Purnima and as the Gaudiya Vaishnav festival in West Bengal. People apply red colour (the colour of passion) to Krishna's idol and then distribute the red coloured powder to family and friends. Holi signifies that our attention should be diverted for the attainment of Krishna and also for the benefit of society. Spring commences from this festival.

In Uttar Pradesh, a special puja known as Holi Milan is performed as people visit every house, sing holi songs and convey their gratitude by putting coloured powder.

Kumaonis have a tradition of singing songs at various times in the day based on ragas such Peelu, Sarang etc. In the evening songs are based on the ragas like Shyamkalyan, Yaman etc.

The youth enjoy the festival particularly playing with the holi colours. Folk songs and dances to the tune of dholak are common.

Dhuleti, which falls the day after Holi Puja, is considered to be the actual festival of colours. Holi is a means for the people to ventilate the feelings of people of various sections and have physical relaxation. The festival of Holi is a time when all of families, neighbours and friends get together. The colourful holi symbolizes one's love for all human beings. The festival of Holi is a time when all disputes and fights get dissolved in love and joy to celebrate the festival and that results in strengthening the feeling of oneness and love. In the evenings bonfires are common on the streets to cleanse the air of evil spirits.

Holi is the end of the year as it is in the end of Phalgun. Planning for the next year begins with the Panchang in the evening.

Holi marks the agricultural season (rabi crop). It is also time for spring harvest. The new crop fills the household and as such this abundance accounts for the celebration. That is why it is also known as 'Vasant Mahotsava', Madanotsav and 'Kama Mahotsava'.

In some parts of India the entire family or at least the head of the family fasts and pray to Krishna and Agni. Krishna's idol is smeared with gulal and "bhog" is offered to both Krishna and Agni.

Dhak or Palash flowers are used to make colours (this is not the case nowadays). The change of weather can cause cold. The use of natural coloured powders to throw on others it is believed have medical benefits. The colours are made of Haldi, Kumkum, Neem and various other leaves such as Bilva and such herbs advised originally by ayurvedic doctors. Flowers of Palash (flame of the forest) are boiled and soaked in water over night to produce yellow coloured water, which is said to have medicinal properties. The colours are also called gulal. These flowers, bright red or deep orange in colour, were collected from the forest and spread out on mats, to dry in the sun, and then ground to fine dust. Colours made from natural coloured talc were used as Holi colours which are good for the skin. Today, however, coloured chemicals are also in use. A drink called thandai is prepared with rich ingredients such as dry fruits and flower petals.

Holi Purnima is also the birthday of Chaitanya Mahaprabhu celebrated mainly in Bengal, but also in Mathura, Vrindavan and Orissa.

Holi spiritually signifies the burning of pride, jealousy, anger, greed, lust and hatred and all such negativities and tendencies within us i.e. the victory of righteousness over demonic forces. Religious observances like fasting or pooja are few. An image of Holika with child Prahlada on her lap is also kept on a log for burning. Combustible items make up Holika's idol but Prahlada's idol is made of materials rather difficult to burn. Twigs of trees and combustible materials are used to throw on to the log of wood. Coconuts are thrown into the bonfire. The ashes from the bonfire are collected the next day and applied on to the limbs of the body. On Phalguna Purnima, Mantras of the Rigveda are chanted to ward off all evil spirits in some parts of India.

Gajendra Moksham

Lord Vishnu came down to earth to protect Gajendra, an Elephant from Makara, a crocodile and gave him moksha. Moksha means salvation. Gajendra then attained the similar four-armed form (Saroopya Mukti) of God and went to Vaikuntha with Vishnu.

***

Sri Krishna

Prayers to Sri Krishna

Vasudeva Sutam Devam Kamsa Chanura Mardanam Devaki Paramaanandam Krishnam Vande Jagadgurum

I salute Lord Krishna, the teacher of the universe, the son of Vasudeva, the destroyer of Kamsa and Chanura, the supreme joy of Devaki.

Om Shree Krishnaya Namaha

I prostrate to Lord Krishna

Om Namo Bhagavate Vaasudevaaya
Srikrishna Govinda Hare Murare He Nath Narayana Vaasudeva
Mukam Karoti Vaachalam Pangum Langhayate Girim
Yat Kripaa Tamaham Vande Paramaananda Maadhavam

I salute that Madhava, the source of supreme bliss, whose grace makes the dumb eloquent and the cripple cross mountain.

Achyutam Keshavam Raamanaarayanam
Krishna Damodaram Vaasudevam Harim
Shridharam Maadhavam Gopika Vallabham
Janaki Naayakam Ramachandram Bhaje

I worship Achyuta, Keshava, Rama, Narayana, Krishna, Damodara, Vasudeva, Hari, Sridhara, Madhava, the beloved of the gopis, the Lord of Sita, Sri Ramachandra.

Maha Mantra
Hare Raama Hare Raama Raama Raama Hare Hare
Hare Krishna Hare Krishna Krishna Krishna Hare
Hare

Man – mind, Tra – deliverance, Maha – great. Maha Mantra means the great deliverance of the mind. The word Hare is a form of addressing the energy of the Lord. The three words Hare, Rama and Krishna are transcendental seeds of the Maha Mantra and the chanting is a spiritual call for the Lord and his internal energy.

About Sri Krishna

Krishna was the eighth avatar of Vishnu. Krishna means attractive ("one who attracts"), dark one. He was born on Janmashtami (also called Gokulashtami) as the 8th son of Devaki and Vasudev in Mathura (sweet). There are various dates mentioned about his birth but was over 5000 years ago.

Krish also means Truth, to be and Na means Bliss (Anand), final emancipation. There is another meaning as well. Krishna means dark. Man does not know the self within and is in the dark. Krishna is dark outside and full of light within. Some texts refer to him as having the colour of rain clouds.

Krishna was born to Devaki and Vasudeva. Kamsa was his uncle. Vasu means prana, Devaki the body and Kamsa the Ego within. He was brought up by Yashoda and Nand. Yash also means fame and Nand means Happiness.

He is known as a Purnavatara as he had all the 16 rays of consciousness. He was handsome, embodiment of beauty with an enchanting smile, his blue colour signifies vastness, infiniteness. The sky, ocean and other vast things are blue in colour. Anything immeasurable looks blue.

His dress is yellow (pitambara). The earth when introduced into a colourless flame produces a yellow hue. Yellow represents the Earth. So the blue form in a yellow dress symbolizes infinite consciousness descended on earth to play a human role.

The incarnation of Krishna represents the descent of the supreme spirit into the world. He is Purushottama – the Supreme. He has the 6 wealths of beauty, fame, wealth, renunciation, knowledge and strength.

The flute is hollow and empty and allows divine breath to go through. The unstuck sounds and the vibrations of prana can be heard. Also the human body is insentient just like the flute and cannot play music on its own, but like the holes the sense organs can allow consciousness to express itself. Flute is the symbol of the Pranava.

The flute is hollow – so when man empties himself of desires and passions, divinity flows through him providing immense bliss. Flute spreads melody of love to people. It is also the sound of a chakra and is heard during meditation. The seven holes represent the seven chakras. When our emptiness is filled with divine music of seven notes (swaras), worldly delusions are overcome.

Krishna dived deep into the river Yamuna to kill Kaliya, the mighty snake. The river represents the mind which is always flowing, and the poisons are the passions and desires coming out of the many hoods and tongues of the snake. Krishna is the consciousness within oneself that vitalises one's thoughts. The lake represents the mind, the snake's hoods are its various passions and desires. So when a man dives deep into the lake of his mind and overcomes the ego, desires and passions, he realises supreme bliss. The sense objects become subservient to the realised soul as he becomes open to reality. The snake also symbolizes alertness.

He lifted the Govardhan mountain when he was seven years old and when eight years old he performed the Maharas during which Radha and the other gopis were drawn into an ecstatic divine state. His leelas / activities are mentioned in Srimad Bhagavatam (the beautiful book of God).

Krishna represents the Self while the gopis represent thoughts. The consciousness is sakshi (witness) and unaffected by the thoughts. The gopis were completely engrossed in Krishna. This way one has to dedicate oneself completely to God, remain unaffected and continue the day to day activity with God in the background in all actions is Karma Yoga. When man works with this spirit, slowly desires lose their significance. Close association with the gopis represents total involvement in Krishna within. Krishna represents the atman in man or the witness within us. The gopis were rishis in their previous lives waiting for final emancipation.

With single pointed devotion our energy gets spiritualised. His crown is a peacock feather i.e. the crown is light and colourful. Supreme knowledge is not burdensome or heavy. With supreme knowledge all daily activities can become light.

Symbolically, if life is milk, it is the process of churning through which you get butter (saintliness). The churning of the butter by the gopis is symbolic of the elimination of vasanas (attachments) and desires and what remains is only longing for the supreme.

Krishna is fond of the mind of the saints like clarified butter. Radha represents the state of devotion that allows one to merge with God in his or her thoughts. It is the flow of devotion to the universal cause and its longing for the supreme spirit. Radha symbolizes the Jivatma (Individual Soul) and Krishna the Paramatma (Supreme Spirit) for which the Jivatma is longing to get that something which can give supreme satisfaction.

Krishna has a garland of 5 colours. It is called Vyjayanti representing five chakras. The five conches (Panchajanya, Anantavijaya etc.) also represent the five chakras. The chains breaking in the prison after his birth signifies that the infinite can never be constrained or restricted even in human form.

Ganga became pure by washing his feet. He gave the Bhagavad Gita to the world – the milk of Upanishads – through his dialogue between Krishna and Arjuna. He is known by several other names. Brijwasi – resident of Brij (Vraj), Gopal – protector of knowledge, Mohana – captivating, Muralidahara - holder of the flute. Govinda, Vinda – one who pleases, Go – earth, cows, senses, praised by the gods, who confers the Vedas. Hrishikesha – lord of the senses, Madhava – also consort of Ma, Janardana – who destroys the wicked, Keshava – who has lovely locks of hair and killer of Keshi, Madhusudhana – sweet like honey and killer of demon Madhu, Kamalanayan – one with lotus eyes.

On Janmashatami day we have to observe Dharma (righteousness), Sharanagati (surrender), Gopi Bhav (devotion) and Satsang (Company of the wise).

There are five attributes of devotion i.e. Shanti bhav (Prahlada), Sakhya bhav (attitude of friendship – Arjuna and Sudama), Vatsalya (parental love – Yashoda for Krishna), Kanta bhav (detached love of Radha and the gopis), Dasya Bhav (like a devoted person to someone higher – e.g. Hanuman). Krishna represents Peace (Shanti) and love (Prema).

Raksha Bandhan

The Hindu festival 'Raksha Bandhan' (knot of protection) came into existence about 6000 years ago, a festival to celebrate the love of a sister for her brother. It is celebrated on the full moon day of Shravan (Raksha = protection Bandhan = tie). Rakhi is considered a strong bond that binds a most beautiful relationship in a relationship of love, affection and trust. The festival's social significance is that everyone should live in harmony with each other. This is the day when the sisters pray for a long life of their brothers and ask God to bless them.

Brothers give them rakhi gifts and promise to care for them as long as they live. Ladies try to make the day special - they buy rakhis, gifts, rakhi pooja thalis and sweets for making the day special. All members of the family get together to celebrate this festival. Presenting Rakhis to brothers and the brothers in turn giving gifts on this occasion makes the event filled with sweet memories for years to come.

Alexander the great of Macedonia was shaken by the bravery of King Puru in his first attempt to conquer India. Alexander's wife was very upset at this. She had heard of the Rakhi festival, and approached King Puru. King Puru accepted her sentiment and he refrained from harming Alexander during the war.

Several hundred years ago, Rajputs faced Muslim invasions. Rakhi was always meant to form a sort of spiritual binding and the promise for the protection of sisters was foremost. Rani Karnawati, the Queen of Chittor who was a widow could not defend her kingdom. She sent a rakhi to Emperor Humayun. Humayun was touched by her gesture and went immediately with his troops to protect her against the invasion of Bahadur Shah, the Sultan of Gujarat whom in no way the Rani could match on her own.

Krishna killed the evil King Sishupal. Krishna was mildly injured during the war. When Draupadi saw his fingers with blood she tore a piece of her sari and tied it to his wrist to stop the bleeding. The Lord was obviously touched by her love and affection. He promised to protect her in future in case a need arises. He thus helped her when the Kauravas were disrobing her; Krishna helped her by elongating her sari so much that it became impossible to disrobe her.

Mahabali, a demon king was a devotee of Vishnu. Vishnu decided to protect Bali's Kingdom and left Vaikuntha. Goddess Lakshmi did not appreciate this as she wanted the Lord to be with her. So she went to Bali in a disguise as a brahmin woman and stayed in his palace. She later tied Rakhi to King Bali on Shravan poornima. Later Lakshmi revealed who she is to the king. Bali was touched by her and Lord Vishnu's affection towards him. Bali then requested Lord Vishnu to take her back to Vaikunta.

The festival is hence known as Baleva representing the importance of Bali's devotion to the Lord.

Brutra, a demon king was advancing in a war between the devatas and the asuras. The devatas who were led by Indra were on the verge of defeat. Indra asked Brihaspati for help. At the suggestion of Brihaspati, Indra had a sacred thread tied on his wrist done amidst the chanting of mantras on this Purnima. Sachi (Indra's wife) tied it on to his hand on that day. The protective power (raksha) of the sacred thread helped the devas win the battle.

In India our festivals are based on seasons and their significance on the people. The festival can be traced back to the Puranic times. Raksha Bandhan was regularly followed for Yama by his sister Yamuna. Yama was moved by her affection and sisterly love. He declared that a boy who gets a rakhi from his sister will be protected.

Lord Krishna asked Yudhishthira to have the Rakhi ceremony for protection against the consequences of the Mahabharat war. Draupadi had tied a rakhi to Lord Krishna.

Rakhis and delicious sweets are prepared for Shravan Purnima. A puja thali consists of rakhi threads, tilak. rice grains, agarbattis, diyas and sweets. First a pooja is done for the family deity. Then the sister performs aarti of her brothers and ties Rakhi on their wrists. She then applies kumkum powder on the forehead of her brothers and offers sweets. All these rituals take place amidst chants meaning – Just like the sun which spreads its sunlight, the radish its seeds, I tie the rakhi to my brother and pray for his long health - and "I tie the rakhi to you, one which was also tied to king Bali to protect you always and never fail you). The brothers promise to protect the sisters from any evil effects of this world".

Rakhi was used just for protection for anyone close and our history has seen many such examples. A rakhi could be tied by wife, a daughter or mother. The Rishis tied rakhi to the devotees who came for blessings. People also tied rakhi to their neighbours and close friends, symbolic of co-existence of every individual. Rabindranath Tagore used the Rakhi utsav to promote unity among all sections of society. Over the years this has become more famous and connected with the brother-sister relationship.

Santoshi Mata's creation on Raksha Bandhan day, is also popular. Ganesh's sister tied a rakhi on Ganesh's wrist. Ganesh's two sons, Shubh and Labh wanted a sister. The sons asked Ganesh and his two wives, Riddhi and Siddhi, for a sister. Ganesh agreed and Santoshi Ma emerged from the divine flames that were created by Riddhi and Siddhi.

People perform the ceremonies and rituals required for Avani Avittam or Upakarma in some parts of India. Balarama, Krishna's elder brother was born on this day. Hindus wear a new sacred thread on this day and offer oblations of water to the ancient Rishis, and the process followed is known as Upakarma. This purnima is the one when the sacred thread Jandhyam, Janeu or Janyo is ceremonially changed.

Oblations of water are also offered to our ancestors, to whom we owe our birth; to the great Rishis, to whom we owe the spiritual knowledge and to the Vedas. It is custom to have sacred threads that are charged with sacred mantras and sanctified with rice, grass (durva) etc. to have these tied by people who know the scriptures and vedic texts or by near and dear ones.

Purnima means a full moon night.The festival is known as Rakhi Purnima in North India and Gamha Purnima in Orissa. Krishna and Radha enjoyed in Shravan – the rainy season ending on Rakhi Purnima. Radha-Krishna idols are swung on decorated swings known as Jhulan Yatra.

The rainy season begins from Nariyal purnima which is celebrated in Maharashtra, Gujarat, and Goa. The fishermen make offerings of coconuts as a mark of gratitude to Varun dev for a good catch of fish.

In Madhya Pradesh, Chattisgarh, Jharkand and Bihar this day is known as Kajari Purnima and in Gujarat as Pavitropana. People worship and do a pooja of Lord Shiva on this day.

Raakhi signifies not mere personal protection of a female. It implies a social life with safety and harmony. Ideally all people must look upon themselves as brothers and sisters as children of the motherland. There is a popular Hindi song 'bhaiya mere, rakhi ke bandhan ko nibhaana'.

Rakhis are nowadays decorated with soft silky threads of various colours, and also with ornaments, pictures, gold and silver threads etc. These Rakhis are made in different shapes, colours to please all sections of people. However, they contain the sacred feelings and well wishes of those who tie the rakhi.

Nowadays pictures of deities are seen on rakhis. After use the rakhi is thrown away and this must be avoided. The rakhi is to be immersed in water.

Sri Krishna Janmaashtami

Lord Krishna is a venerated avatar who came on earth over 5000 years ago. Janmastami (also known as Krishnastami or Gokulastami) is a festival dedicated to Krishna and commemorates his birth and comes sometime in August. This was in the month of Sharavan on the 8th day of the second lunar fortnight.

This first day is Krishnastami, also called Gokulastami. The next day is known as Janmastami. Krishna was born on Wednesday (Rohini Nakshatra).

The first day is celebrated until midnight as the birth of the Lord. On the second day there is a celebration of breaking a pot full of milk or butter (Dahi Handi). Krishnastami has become very popular with this ceremony. An earthen pot is filled with milk, honey, yoghurt, butter, fruits and other items and is suspended at a height of 15 to 40 feet from a rope between buildings or trees. A pyramid of people is formed by persons standing over each other on their shoulder. The person who reaches the top, claims the contents of the pot after breaking it. Krishna's love for milk and butter is replicated through this event. When Krishna was a young boy, he and his friends together used to get into the houses in his area and nearby in search of milk and butter. In the olden days food stuff used to be put in a pot suspended from the roof so as to prevent cats, dogs and other domesticated animals from spoiling the items. Sweets are prepared from milk and curds which Krishna loved. Janmaashtami is celebrated with enormous zeal and enthusiasm. It is a practise to visit many places and try to to break as many handis as possible. In the olden days such people were referred to as govindas on this day.

Cattle are one of the principal means of subsistence in an agricultural society and therefore the activity of people revolves around taking care of cows, milking them, making curds, butter etc. prevalent at that time. Govinda and Gopala are shouted as they also mean cowherd. In Sanskrit one of the meanings of Go is cow; it also means knowledge. Vasudeva represents Vedas and Devaki the Omkara. Krishna is the truth manifested by the Vedas and the Omkara. This truth kills the Kamsa (Ego and Conflict).

Hindus fast on Saptami, the seventh day which is followed by a night-long vigil commemorating the birth of Krishna at midnight in the jail. Shri Krishna's uncle

Kansa had kept Vasudev and Devaki in a prison. His father had taken him to Nand's house for the safety of the newly born Krishna. People observe Nirjala Vrat for the whole day and night, or at least fast for the day and have fruits and milk at night. They may be awake at night (jagran) with the night spent singing Bhajans and Kirtans. The fast is broken after aarti and prayers are conducted.

Ladies draw children's footstep prints outside which are done with rice-flour. This is to symbolize the coming of the infant Krishna into their homes.

Rasaleelas are a special feature in Mathura, Vrindavan and also in Manipur. The Rasa lila and the Dahi Handi celebrate Krishna's playfulness in his younger days. This tradition is known as Uriadi in Tamil Nadu.

Lord Krishna's idol is placed in a decorated mantap in Karnataka and snacks and sweets specially prepared for the festival are offered to Krishna along with fruits. In Karnataka, they prepare avalakki and bellada panaka for the festival. Chaklis are also made. Avalakki is prepared in memory of Sudhama who had once offered it to Krishna, who considered it to be one of his favourite snacks.

In Mathura, Uttar Pradesh (Krishna's birthplace), Gokul and Vrindavan celebrations go up to a week. In Dwarka (Gujarat) the Dwarkadhish temple celebrates it with great joy. Music and dance mark the celebration of this festival in North India. At midnight, the statue of infant

Krishna is bathed and placed in a rocking cradle amidst the ringing of bells.

Pravachans from Bhagavatam are done from the 10th Skandha which deals with past times of Krishna. The next day is called Nanda Utsav or the joyous celebration of Nanda Maharaj and Yashoda.

The birthday of Lord Krishna is very special for Hindus as we consider him an incarnation of God. The celebration is colourful particularly in places where Krishna was born and lived as a young boy. Rasa leela is performed to relive the incidents in the life of Krishna and to respect his love for Radha. Devotees chant the mantra *Om Namo Bhagavate Vaasudevaaya.*

The Bhagavatam is considered equal to the Upanishads as they reveal the glory of Krishna and his Lilas. Krishna's avatar was for achieving the following: destroying the wicked demons, playing an important in the battle of Kurukshetra (delivering of the Bhagavad Gita) and the development of bhakti in India. He lived his teachings and was great in knowledge and action. The Name, virtues, and Lilas of Krishna are to be remembered and meditated upon. One can also meditate on the Lotus feet of Radha and Krishna. Devotion kindles love for the Lord, who eventually frees man from the bondage of samsara.

Krishna was exemplary is all the roles he played during his incarnation – as Arjuna's friend and charioteer in the Mahabharata war, as a musician, as a playful boy and cowherd in Vrindavan and Gokul, statesman, and the deliverer of the Bhagavad Gita. He taught Narada the art of playing the veena. His flute enthralled the Gopis. He showed divine powers even as a child by killing many demons. He revealed his cosmic form to His mother, Yashoda. The Rasa Leela, the secret of which could only be understood by devotees like Narada, Radha and the Gopis was performed by him. He revealed the supreme truth to Arjuna and Uddhava through the Bhagavad Gita and the Uddhav Gita. He mastered all the sixty-four fine arts. He is the only one who is regarded as a complete avatar and who had all the rays of consciousness.

In times when there is the rise of extreme cruelty and unrighteousness and when the societal values very badly deteriorate the Lord incarnates to re-establish righteousness and peace.

The incarnations usually come with their companions. Lord Rama came with his brothers. Krishna came with Balarama and Rishis. Some, like Chaitanya, are born to instil devotion in the hearts of people and turn their minds towards God. An avatar such as Krishna comes rarely only when there is widespread disorder in the world. The scriptures have perhaps not recorded any avatar's life more completely than the life of Lord Krishna.

Krishna has said the he alone existed prior to creation and that he is that which will remain after dissolution. Maya (illusion) has no purpose and can't be found in the Self. Krishna said he pervades the entire universe and is also separate from it.

All of us must realise that the Supreme exists, is omnipresent and eternal. We can experience this only in a super-conscious state. Then there is no duality of maya experienced and nothing any longer disturbs the devotee.

Lord Krishna has mentioned to Yudhishtira that Janmashtami is an important day to celebrate (please refer to the Bhavihyottara Puran). He incarnated to defeat the evil King Kansa who was harassing his people. His also had to fulfil the promise he had given to Vasudev and Devaki. King Kansa had heard a divine voice proclaiming that their eighth son would kill Kansa. Kansa imprisoned Vasudev and Devaki. He also killed the first seven sons born to them. Vasudev carried the baby Krishna in the cradle through the Yamuna river. Thus the Krishna's death was thus avoided and he eventually killed vanquished Kansa.

The first importance of Janmashtami is to observe dharma. All humans are imprisoned in their thoughts and the cycles of births and deaths. Krishna incarnated in this prison, to establish dharma and redeem living beings from maya. It is clear that one can win over maya with the support of Krishna. Arjuna did this when he sought Krishna's support during the Mahabharata war. The Lord essence of his sermons in the Gita – O Arjuna, forsake all your beliefs and surrender to me – I will deliver you from all sins. Surrendering to the Lord's feet is the spirit of Janmashtami.

Brahmarup means to become an ideal devotee. Arjuna is a good example of this. This is the relationship of a human (Nar) and God (Narayan). This is why we find murtis of Nar-Narayan during the festival. Krishna's Ras Leela. Devotees need to develop 'Gopi-bhav', like Radha to worship Krishna. Devotees consecrate murtis of 'Radha-Krishna' in temples, for worshipping Radha-Krishna.

Shri Krishna advocated 'Satsang', while celebrating Janmashtami. Krishna said in the Bhagavad Gita "I am not as pleased by efforts of Yoga, Sankhya, scriptural study, sacrifice, renunciation, charity, fasting, yagnas, study of scriptures, following the laws of Dharma and Yama (Patanjali's eightfold path), as I am by Satsang". Satsang means association with a Satguru and this is an important aspect of the festival.

Deepavali

Deepavali known as the "festival of lights", is an important five-day festival (for some three days) celebrated in mid-October/November. The name Deepavali - 'Deepa' means diya (a clay lamp pot) or light and 'Avali', means a row – meaning a row of lamps to signify the victory of good over evil. The word "Diwali" is a shorter version of "Deepavali". Diwali is one of the important festivals in India and one which is celebrated with great fervour. This is the great festival to honour Goddess Lakshmi. It is on a new moon day in the month of Ashwin.

Many significant events are associated with Diwali. It commemorates the return of Lord Rama, Sita and Lakshmana, from their fourteen-year-long exile after defeating the demon-king Ravana. The people of Ayodhya (where he was born and it was also his Kingdom's capital) illuminated the kingdom with diyas (oil lamps) and burst firecrackers in a joyous celebration.

Dhanteras is the first day on which many business communities begin their new financial year. On Dhanteras people clean their houses and light lamps in the evening. Goddess Lakshmi (goddess of wealth) is invoked for wealth.

Lord Dhanvantari of Ayurveda (God of medicine) emerged from the samudra manthan with a kalash filled with Amrit that confers immortality. Hindus pray to Lord Yama (the god of death) on this day. The medical profession considers the day as important for healing (the Ayurvedic doctors).

The second day is Naraka Chaturdasi which was the day the demon Naraka was defeated by Krishna and his wife Satyabhama and later killed by Krishna. The belief is that fasting on this day helps one move towards heaven.

Amavasya (new moon day) is the third day of Deepavali, marks the worship of Lakshmi to fulfil our wishes. Lord Vishnu in his dwarf incarnation as Vamana vanquished Bali and sent him to Patal lok. On the fourth day of Deepavali (padyami) Bali went to Patal and took the reins of his new kingdom there.

The fifth day called Bhai Dooj or Bhaubeej or Yama Dvitiya. The brothers visit their sisters houses to express their love and affection for each other. There is a story that Yama visited his sister Yami on this day. Yami (the river Yamuna) welcomed him with an Aarti and enjoyed the day together as a feast. Yama gave a gift to Yami for her affection. This day is therefore also called Yama Dwitiya.

The day after Diwali is for Govardhan Puja. This is the day Krishna defeated Indra. Indra (god of rain) had to accept that Krishna as the supreme.

There are many other historical events that happened on this day. The Pandavas had returned after 12 years of exile in the forest (Vanvas) and one year of agyatavas (where they lived incognito). King Vikramaditya was coronated on this day.

In each of the above events and legends the common factor of Deepavali lies in the victory of good over evil. The move of our self from darkness into light – the light that empowers us to perform good deeds and which helps us to become closer to the divine. During Deepavali the streets are lit by lamps and the scent of incense sticks evident all around along with the sounds of the joy of bursting fire-crackers.

The significance of the lamps is to make us aware of the inner light within us. Hindus believe that there is a pure, infinite, and eternal consciousness called the Atman beyond the body/mind complex. Deepavali refers to the light of knowledge which dispels ignorance, for we are not merely the body, but also the infinite reality. It is an awakening that needs to take place in all and this generates compassion, happiness and knowledge of the oneness of all things. The festival is to celebrate the development of this inner light.

Govatsa Dwadashi (also known as Vasu Baras) – Go: for cow and vatsa: meaning calf. Dwadashi means the 12th day – the cow and calf are worshipped. King Prithu, was the son of the tyrant King Vena whose rule was bad for the people. There was a terrible famine and earth was no longer fruitful. Prithu chased the earth, represented as cow, and 'milked' her, signifying that he brought prosperity to his kingdom.

Dhanatrayodashi or Dhanteras or also known as Dhanwantari Triodasi; Dhan stands for wealth and Trayodashi, the 13th day. It is considered a good day for purchase of gold. Chaturdashi means the 14th day. The demon Narakasura was killed by Krishna on this day. These killings of demons by Gods signify the victory of good over evil. Also the victory of light over darkness. People wake up before or around dawn, have an oil bath and dress up in new clothes. Lamps are then lit all around the house. Beautiful kolams /rangolis are drawn outside the homes. A special pooja is performed for Krishna. The Lord liberated the world from the demon Narakasura. Taking a bath before sunrise is believed to be healthy. After the puja children burn fire crackers heralding the defeat of the demon. The usual festivity of relatives and family members meeting and celebrating is evident. The external explosion is meant to diffuse the internal stresses.

In North India, people perform Lakshmi pooja and Ganesh Pooja for an auspicious beginning. Lamps are lit in the streets and in homes to welcome prosperity. Lakshmi emerged from Kshira Sagar during the great churning of the ocean (Samudra manthan) on this day. Lord Vamana (a Vishnu avatar) killed Bali on this day.

On this day, Vishnu came back to Vaikuntha, his abode. On this day Lakshmi-panchayatan (group of five) enters the universe, so those who worship Lakshmi receive her grace and devotees are blessed with physical and mental well-being. Vishnu (Happiness), Indra (happiness due to wealth), Kubera (wealth), Gajendra (carrier of the wealth) and Lakshmi are the members of this group. Lakshmi is the divine Energy which provides shakti to all the above activities.

By the time the Deepavali festival comes harvest season ends in many parts of India. Farmers are grateful for the produce last year and pray for a good harvest in the coming year. Lakshmi symbolizes the eight types of wealth including wealth and prosperity, and we seek her blessings for a good year ahead. In Bengal they worship goddess Kali.

This festivity brings about unity. It instils charity in the hearts of people. This is also time for new clothes for the family and to forgive others. It brings in lot of excitement across all the sections of society irrespective of their socio-economic background. Business families close their accounts and pray for prosperity during the ensuing year. Employers give gifts for their employees. People celebrate with an exchange of sweets. The fireworks are symbolic of the effigies of Narakasura killed on this day.

In the earlier days people used to get up early for bath and massage the body with of oil, flour and haldi (turmeric) before the daily bath. Waking up at Brahmamuhurta (at 4 a.m.) serves a great blessing for spiritual advancement. In the evening tarpan (offering oblations of water) is offered to Yama.

In traditional vedic culture four festivals (parvas) are celebrated, namely, Upakarma, Vijaydashami, Deepavali and Holi. The festivals commence with Upakarma (Raksha-bandhan) and end with Holi. Each of them is associated with a different goddess. Raksha-bandhan (Goddess Saraswati); Vijaydashami with Devi or Shakti); Holi with Prasannata and Deepavali with Lakshmi.

The message of "Tamaso ma jyotir gamaya" (lead me from from darkness unto light) is message of the festival. The burning diyas signify the destruction of the gap between the rich and poor – destruction of discrimination based on the wealth levels of the poor and the rich. The diya is a symbol of this unity.

Another message of the lighting diyas of Deepavali is "Let us provide what is needed to help so that neighbour's lamps can be lit". One candle or a lamp can light many candles. Also a small amount of charity can bring joy to the poor. Placing diyas (lamps) inside and around the home marks Deepavali. The lamps are displayed at the entrance and on the compound walls on the streets symbolising that the inner light of an individual must radiate outside. Feeding the underpriviledged and joy for the poor is the true spirit of Deepavali and the true prayer to Goddess Lakshmi.

The magnificent five days celebrations are marked by multi-coloured rangoli designs, an array of lamps, floral decorations, fireworks, exchange of Diwali Sweets and Diwali Gifts. The glowing lamps welcome Lakshmi, the Goddess of wealth and prosperity. The house is lit with lamps, but the heart in some of us has the darkness of ignorance. Hence we pray "lead me from darkness to light".

Kamadhenu

Kamadhenu, is a divine bovine-goddess in Hindu mythology as the mother of all cows. She is a miraculous cow which provides her owner what he desires. Hindus respect cows as the embodiment of the Kamadhenu. Cows are worshipped during the Raksha Bandhan and Deepavali festivals. Donation of a cow (Godan) was done to a family to sustain their living. India was and is largely an agrarian society.

***

Sri Rama

Ram, Lakshman, Sita and Hanuman

Prayers to Sri Rama

Om Sriraama Raama Raameti Rame Raame Mano Rame
Sahasranaama Tattulyam Raama Naama Varaanane

I delight in the beautiful name of Sri Rama again and again for even once remembered, the name of Sri Rama bestows the fruit equal to the thousand names of Lord Vishnu.

Apadaamapa Hartaram
Dataaram Sarvasampadaam
Lokaabhiraamam Sriraamam
Bhuyo Bhuyo Namamyaham

I bow again and again to Sri Rama who is the remover of all misfortunes, the giver of prosperity and who is the beloved of the whole universe.

Ramaaya Raama Bhadraaya
Raamachandraaya Vedhase
Raghunathaaya Nathaaya
Sitaayaa Pathaye Namaha

Salutations to the Lord Rama who is present in all beings as Rama, Ramabhadra and Ramachandra, the Lord of the Raghu Vamsa, the husband of Sita.

Om Shree Ram Jaya Ram Jaya Jaya Ram

Om Shree Rama. Victory to Rama, Victory to Rama.

About Sri Rama

Rama was an incarnation of Vishnu and came as an avatar to display to humanity the role of an ideal human being, obedient son, devoted brother, trusted friend and noble enemy. He was an ideal man, son and king. Sita his consort, an incarnation of Lakshmi was an ideal daughter, wife, queen and mother. Rama was an ideal of perfection and an example for spiritual conduct. Rama is the central figure of the epic Ramayana. Sita personifies the ideal social and sacred relationship between man and woman. The Rama Mantra (also known as Taraka mantra) enables one to cross the ocean of Life or Samsara. He stood for righteousness. The bows and arrows symbolize readiness to fight injustice.

Rama was the seventh incarnation of Vishnu. Ra means radiant and Ma means self. Rama means one who is radiant within oneself. Rama is the in-dweller in everybody. Shiva tells Parvati repetition of the name Rama is equal to the repetition of the Lord's name or a mantra one thousand times. The Ramarahasyopanishad says Rama is a combination of the essence of the Narayana (of the Ashta-Akshara mantra) – Ra and the Shiva-Pancha-Akshara-Ma.

The others associated with Rama in Ramayana represent persons completely devoted to dharma. Lakshmana represents intellect and a symbol of sacrifice, Sugriva discrimination and Vali despair. Dasaratha represents intellect that controls the senses and organs of action, his three wives representing the three gunas, the four sons the four goals of life. Kausalya means skilled. When the five sense organs and the five organs of action are used skilfully, radiance is born within. The three rakshasas personify the three gunas – Ravana (Rajas), Kumbakarna (Tamas) and Vibhishana (Sattva). Sita is purity personified and fully aware despite the travails of life. Rama represents Satya (Truth) and Dharma (Righteousness).

Ramayana exemplifies the importance of righteousness in the life of a human being. The demons represent evil propensities.

Sri Rama Navami

Rama Navami is the birthday of Lord Rama, the seventh incarnation of Vishnu. He was born in Ayodhya. Rama Navami is celebrated on the ninth day of Hindu month of Chaitra (usually in March/April). Rama Navami marks the end of nine days festival known as Vasanta Navratri. The day is considered auspicious and devotees observe fasting, visit temples to offer prayers, takes religious processions and pravachans (lectures/preachings) on Ramayana are also held. Lord Rama was a descendent of the Ikshvaku race.

Lord Rama is revered as a maryada purushottam or adarsha purusha. He symbolized morality and was the ideal son, husband and king. Rama is also remembered for his prosperous and righteous reign during his period known as Rama Rajya. Rama was a legendary person known for his chivalry, righteousness, heroic deeds and virtue and these have inspired people for thousands of years. He set the example of an ideal human being an example for others to follow. Rama Rajya, the rule of Rama was a rare duration of peace and prosperity.

Rama Navami vrat is considered to be one of the five most important vratas since ancient times.

In some states the festival lasts for the nine days of the Navratri and hence called 'Sri Rama Navratri'. It is marked by continuous recitals or Akhanda Rama Nama Sankirtan and the Ramacharitamanas. Bhajans, kirtans are sung and distribution of prasad takes place after the puja and aarti. Infant Rama's idols are kept on cradles and rocked by devotees.

Rama was born at noon and hence temples are decorated and prayers are held in the morning. Havans are organized in temples along with chanting of Vedic mantras. Fruits and flowers are offered. Many followers fast during this day and follow this by sweets in the evening. Along with Sri Rama, people also worship Sita, Lakshmana, Rama's brother and Hanuman a great devotee of Rama. Sri Rama Navami is dedicated to remembering Rama with bhakti as the Supreme.

In the Bhadrachalam temple they celebrate the wedding anniversary of Rama and Sita. Thousands of devotees visit temples. Rathayatras (the chariot processions) of Rama, Lakshmana and Hanuman, are taken out in the processions to various places surrounding the temples. Many people take a dip in Sarayu, which is considered a sacred river.

Dasharatha had no children for a long time from his three wives, namely, Kausalya, Sumitra and Kaikeyi. They were worried that there would be no heir to the throne in the their (Ikshvaku) lineage. Rishi Vasistha told Dasaratha to perform Puthra Kamesti Yagna to have a child. He recommended that Maharshi Rishyasringa should perform this yagna for him. Emperor Dasharath invited Maharshi who agreed and performed the yagna. Yagneshwara appears as a result and provides Dasharatha with a bowl of divine Kheer and asks him to give it to all his spouses. Dasharata gives half each of the kheer or payasam to Kausalya, the elder of his wives and to Kaikeyi. Each of them give half of what they got to Sumitra. All three Queens eventually conceived. Kausalya gave birth to Rama at mid day on the ninth day of Chaitra. The other children were Bharata to Kaikeyi and twins Lakshmana and Shatrughna to Sumitra.

Vishnu incarnates when Adharma rises in society to re-establish dharma. Rama had incarnated to kill Ravana, an Asura (demon).

Marriage celebrations (Kalyanotsavam) are performed in temples while some people do them at home with small idols of Rama and Sita. The day marks the end of a nine days period of celebration known as Vasanthothsava in South India (Spring festival). It is known as Chaitra Navaratri (in Maharashtra) and starts with Gudi Padwa.

Swaminarayan Jayanti is the birthday of Swaminarayan, a great saint and it also falls on this day.

On Rama Navami, a Ratha Yatra (chariot procession) is taken out, particularly in North India. The procession consists of a beautiful and well decorated chariot on which the persons standing playing the roles of the main characters of Ramayana. In the procession people are dressed up as Rama's soldiers.

There are nine planets in the solar system, nine forms of devotion, nine forms of Durga and hence nine is considered as a very important number. Rama Navami is celebrated remembering nine of Lord Rama's great virtues. Rama had all the virtues and practised what he preached. His heritage, his extraordinary prowess, impeccable character, popularity, courage, compassion, sense of justice, obedience to his parents, and his Guru, intelligence, extraordinary patience, many other such positive traits were loved by the people. Rama was always aware of and meticulously performed his duty. He sacrificed everything in the pursuit of duty. He strictly adhered to dharma until the very end.

Rama was generous and had a willingness to listen and help others with their problems.

Rama fought for the people of his kingdom. He stood his ground for the cause of righteousness. He exhibited bravery. He had a good in understanding combat operations

Rama's key attribute was kindness and compassion. He taught mankind how to be brave and at the same time be compassionate.

Rama's kindness was tempered by his love for justice. Even the poor and humble could voice their views and feelings on issues. He was an embodiment of justice.

Dasharath ordered Rama to take the kingdom by force, imprison him by taking the support of the army. Rama refused such suggestions for he felt that it was a sin to break a promise.

His love and support for all, whether rich or poor, helped him win the hearts of the people.

Ra stands for radiance and Ma for Self. So when one is radiant within oneself the Rama within one is born. Dasharatha signifies the ten – 5 each organs of senses and actions. Kaushalya represents kushalatha meaning skilful application. So when we act with our senses and organs of action skilfully the Rama within us is born. The ideal of self-less service has made Rama one of the greatest heroes of all time. Another meaning is RA+A+MA standing for Surya, Chandra and Agni.

Lord Brahma received complaints from the devatas or gods about the trouble that Ravana was creating. They were helpless as Lord Brahma had granted several boons to Ravan. He could not be killed by a god or deva. Ravana had become overconfident. He did not expect an attack from a human being. Hence, Vishnu agreed to descend on earth as Rama. Ramayana is a popular scripture. It is loved by the people irrespective of caste and creed.

Bhajans praising the story of Lord Rama, his loyal brother Lakshman and his devoted wife Sita are sung. Pictures of Rama, Sita, Lakshman and Hanuman are put on the altar for the puja. Pooja flowers, lamps and incense sticks are kept before the deities. Arti is performed and prasad is distributed. Puranic Dramas on Rama are staged in the evenings.

Ramayana was the first written book in history and also written when the events were going on.

Ugadi/Gudi Padwa

Ugadi in Telugu comes from yuga and aadi, yuga means era, aadi means start. The people of Karnataka and Andhra Pradesh call this festival Ugadi. The festival is the new year's day for people of Andhra Pradesh, Karnataka, Maharashtra and Goa. It falls as per the Saka calendar in the month of Chaitra (March /April on Chaitra Shuddha Padyami) which is the first month in the Indian calendar with Ugadi as the first day and in Maharshtra (Gudi Padwa).

It is believed that Brahma started creation on this day. The great Indian mathematician Bhaskaracharya said the Ugadi day from the sunrise as the beginning of the new year. There is a certain relation to the position of the Sun which is not explained here.

The day begins with bath at or before dawn followed by prayers, and then eating of a mixture of six tastes called

Ugadi Pachhadi in Telugu and Bevu-Bella in Kannada. All experiences in life such as sadness, happiness, anger etc should be accepted without getting overjoyed or perturbed by the nature of the experience. The fresh chutney or pachhadi has neem buds or flowers for bitterness, tamarind juice for sourness, green chilli for heat, raw mango for tang, jaggery and banana pieces for sweetness and salt for saltiness. Members of the family take this mixture as it is believed to help in purifying the blood and strengthen the immune system. In Andhra Pradesh and Karnataka sweet dishes such as Bobbatlu, Obbattu or Holige, and in Maharashtra Puran Poli are prepared.

Mantras are chanted and predictions are made for the new year. People gather to listen to discourses on the Panchangam (almanac) of the new year and the forecast of the year. This is called the 'Panchanga Sravanam', a social function where a respected scholar makes a general predictions for all present to hear based on the new almanac. Nowadays people also watch broadcasts of the "Panchanga Sravanam" on TV.

Literary discussions, poetry recitations (kavi sammelan) and recognition of authors for their literary works take place during social and cultural programs. Awards are also given. Recitals of carnatic music and traditional dance concerts are held in the evenings.

Ugadi/Gudi Padwa comes close to Holi bringing in the freshness of spring. The flame of the forest tree develops foliage and blooms with red flowers. Spring marks a beginning for plants acquiring new leaves. Spring is the first season of the year full of greenery and colours signifying prosperity. Jasmine flowers spread fragrance. Garlands made of Jasmine flowers are placed over the idols in temples. Raw mangoes start spreading their aroma in the environment. Neem trees help cleanse the air. Sweets made with jaggery from new sugarcane crop add flavour to the typical Ugadi dishes.

Ugadi is celebrated with festive fervour in Maharashtra, Karnataka and Andhra Pradesh. They doors of the houses at the entrance are decorated with fresh mango leaves. Karthik (Subrahmanya or Muruga) and Ganesha, the two sons of Siva and Parvathi were fond of mangoes. Karthikeya had suggested to people to put green mango leaves on the doorway implying having a good crop and well-being.

Mango leaves and coconuts (as in a Kalash or Kalasam, to initiate any pooja) are used on auspicious occasions to propitiate gods. In villages people put fresh cow dung water on the ground in front of their houses and then draw rangoli (colourful designs). We invoke the blessings of God before we start the new year. We pray for the health, prosperity and for the success of our businesses. Ugadi is auspicious to start new ventures.

Gudi Padwa is the Marathi name of Chaitra Shukla Pratipada. The word padwa is derived from the Sanskrit word Pratipada for first day of a lunar month after new moon day (Amavasya). Gudi Padwa is Samvatsar Padvo for Konkanis, and in many states in North / Central India as Nav Varsha Samvat, Kashmir (Nav Roz),

Punjab (Baisakhi), Bengal (Naba Barsha), in Assam (Goru Bihu), Tamil Nadu (Puthandu), Sindhis (Cheti Chand). Manipuris, (Sajibu Cheiraoba), and Kerala (Vishu).

Our country has been largely been an agri based economy and hence the festivals have have a linkage to the sowing and reaping seasons. Gudi Padwa falls at the end of the Rabi season.

On this festival day, one can find a "gudi" hanging out of house, window in a house of a Maharashtrian family for all to see. Gudi from which the festival got its name is a bright green or yellow cloth tied to the top of a bamboo over there are items tied such as sugar crystals, neem and mango leaves and garland of red flowers. Usually a copper pot is placed upside down over it.

The gudi symbolizes Brahma's flag (Brahmadhwaj – refer Brahma Purana). The gudi also signifies Rama's victory and return to Ayodhya after killing Ravan. The festival marks the coronation of Rama after his return to Ayodhya after the 14 years of exile. The gudi is believed to ward off evil and invite prosperity into the house. The gudi is placed on the right side of the main entrance of the house.

Women and children work on beautiful rangoli designs at their doors with vibrant colours mirroring the colours associated with spring. Like most other festivals family members wear new clothes. Maharashtrian families make srikhand on this day. Konkanis make Kanangachi Kheer.

***

Lakshmi

Prayers to Lakshmi

Lakshmim Kshira Samudrarajatanayaam Shriranga
Dhameshwarim
Daasi Bhuta Samasta Devavanitaam Lokaika
Deepamkuraam
Shreemanmanda Kataaksha Labhda vibhava
brahmendra Gangadharaam
Twaam Trailokya Kutumbinim Sarasijaam Vande
Mukunda Priyaam

I worship that Lakshmi, the daughter of the king of the milk-ocean, the queen of the abode of the Lord Vishnu, whose servants are the wives of all the gods, who is the one light and the sprout of the universe, through a side glance of whose benign grace Brahma, Indra, Siva have attained their high positions, who is the mother of the three worlds, who is called Kamala and who is the consort of Bhagavan Vishnu.

Ya Devi Sarva Bhuteshu Lakshmi Roopena
Samsthita
Namastasyai Namastasyai Namastasyai Namo
Namaha

I worship again and again Goddess Lakshmi who abides in all beings and bestows good fortune.

Namastestu Mahamayai
Supreete Surapujite
Shankha Chakra Gadahaste
Mahaalakshmi Namostute

I bow to you the great cause of Maya seated on a great throne, Who is worshipped by the gods who holds the conch, discuss and mace in the hand, I bow to you Mahalakshmi.

Om Shree Mahalakshmyai Namaha

About Lakshmi

Lakshmi is the Goddess of wealth, fortune and beauty. She arose as a gift of the churning of the ocean of milk by the gods and asuras (evil forces). The rise from this churning symbolizes absolute purity. She is also referred to as Sri. She is the consort of Vishnu. Lakshya in Sanskrit means goal. Whenever Vishnu descends on the earth as an avatar, she has also accompanied him as Sita, the consort of Rama, Rukmini as consort of Krishna, Padmavathi of Venkateshwara etc.

She is extraordinarily beautiful and is seen sitting or standing on a lotus. She wears a lotus garland. That is why she is also known as Padma or Kamala. She carries lotus flowers in her hands. The blooming lotuses signify the different stages of evolution and ascension from murkiness (lotus blooms from murky water). Lotus also means rooted in supreme reality. Live in the world but not be obsessed with only wealth and desires. The lotus is also floating in water indicating instability of wealth. She carries compassion for humanity.

Her four hands signify the power to provide the values and ends of human life, that is, Dharma (righteousness), Artha (wealth), Kama (desires) and Moksha (self realization). Her right hand shows that she is blessing devotees. The gold coins flowing from her hands indicate that those who worship her will gain wealth. The amruthakalasa symbolises immortality.

Her red dress indicates activity with a gold border implying prosperity. The elephants shown on either side of her sprinkling water on her denotes continuous activity and abundance.

The fruits stand for the benefits of hard work. The universal mother is kind to grant fruits for our labour. Usually a bilva fruit is shown which stands for moksha or liberation. She is referred to as having swarna hasta or golden hands as she provides riches to people. The wealth provided also includes moral and spiritual wealth as opposed to mere material wealth. It includes spiritual wealth for spiritual development.

She is known as Chanchal (restless as wealth may not stay for long), Lokamata (Universal Mother), Haripriya (the beloved of Hari, and Padmalaya (residing on a lotus), Indira (powerful one), Rama (one who gives happiness).

The various forms of Lakshmi representing the eight wealths are Dhana Lakshmi (Wealth and fortune), Dhanya Lakshmi (Food), Dhairya Lakshmi (courage), Vijaya Lakshmi (Success), Santaana Lakshmi (wealth of children), Adi Lakshmi (First, prior wealth), Vidya

Lakshmi (education – not merely normal education but the development of noble characteristics), and Gaja Lakshmi (wealth of animals). She is also known as Rajya Lakshmi (wealth of an empire).

Varalakshmi Vratam

This puja is done by married women seeking the blessings of Varalakshmi. Ladies perform pooja ceremony in the morning in their homes. In the evenings a lot of women are invited for exchange of prasad. Women pray to Varalakshmi who is symbolic of the eight types of wealth for the happiness of the family members, longevity of the husband and for any personal wishes they may have. Vara means boon and it is believed that Varalakshmi grants boons on this day.

The vratam commences on the Friday immediately after the full moon day during the month of Shravan. It can also be performed on any Friday in this month. Shiva has advised us about the glory of this vrat in the Skanda purana. We pray to a kalash representing the Goddess. It is filled with rice and fresh mango leaves, a coconut and cloth are placed on the top of the coconut. Goddess Lakshmi is invoked and worshipped with grains which are symbolic of prosperity.

Mahalakshmi appeared as a Brahmin lady to Charumathi (who lived in Magadh and was considered to be an ideal wife) in her dreams and asked her to perform a pooja to Varalakshmi and stated that her that if she does so her wishes will be granted. The family did as advised by Mahalakshmi and soon their home was filled with riches and jewellery. Charumathi also found a golden chariot waiting outside the house.

Purchase of gold is considered auspicious on this day. Mothers advise their daughters to perform this Vrat every year for their family's overall happiness and for the long life of their husbands.

***

Shiva

Prayers to Shiva

Mahaa Mrityunjaya Mantra
Om Tryambakam Yajaamahe
Sugandhim Pushtivardhanam
Urvaarukamiva Bandhanaan
Mrityormuksheeya Maamritaat

We worship the three eyed Lord Shiva who is fragrant and who nourishes all the beings. May he liberate me from death even as a cucumber is severed from its link to the creeper.

Namaste Asthu Bhagavan Vishweshwaraaya
Mahaadevaaya
Tryambakaaya Tripuraanthakaaya Trikaalaagni
Kalaaya
Kaalaagni Rudraya Neelakanthaaya
Mrytyunjayaaya
Sarveshwaraaya Sadashivaaya Shreeman
mahaadevaaya Namaha

Salutations to Lord Shiva who is the Lord of the universe, who is the all knowing effulgence, who has three eyes, who burnt the city of the three demons, who is in the three periods of time which is like fire, who is timeless and the destroyer of time, whose neck is blue, who has won over death, who is the Lord of all, who is always a blessing, who is endowed with all wealth and who is the great Lord.

**Vande Shambhumumaapatim Suragurum
Vande Jagatkaaranam
Vande Pannagabhooshanam Mrigadharam
Vande Pashoonaam Patim
Vande Soorya Shashaanka Vahnunayanam
Vande Mukundapriyam
Vande Bhaktajanaashrayam Cha Varadaam
Vande Shivam Shankaram**

I prostrate to Lord Shiva, the consort of Uma, who is the teacher of the celestials, who is the ultimate cause of the Universe, who adorns himself with snakes and holds a deer, who is the Lord of all living beings, whose three eyes are the sun, moon and fire, who is very dear to Vishnu, who is the refuge of all devotees, who grants boons, who is auspiciousness and bestows peace.

Om Namah Shivaya

I prostrate to Lord Shiva.

Na – Earth, Mah – Water, Shi – Fire, Va – Air and Ya – Space.

**Karpuragauram Karunaavataaram
Samsaarasaaram Bhujagendrahaaram
Sada Vasantam Hridayaravinde
Bhavam Bhavaani Sahitam Namaani**

I bow to Lord Shiva who is white as camphor, an incarnation of mercy, the essence of the world, who has the king of serpents as his garland, and who always dwells in the lotus of the heart with Goddess Parvati.

About Shiva

Shiva is the third lord of the trinity. He is the one responsible for the dissolution of the universe. Shiva means the auspicious one. Adi Shankara said Shiva is 'the one who purifies everyone by the utterance of his name'. Shiva also indicates the one in whom the creation sleeps after the process of dissolution.

All things born must disintegrate or get destroyed at some stage before the next cycle of birth or creation. The transformative energy principle that brings about this change is Shiva. So actually he is equally responsible for creation. Destruction can also be viewed as a positive force – destruction of evil and as a regenerator, in a positive sense the death of the old personality and old habits.

He is shown usually in a meditative pose besmeared with ashes, with three eyes, with four arms holding a trishul or trident, damaru or drum and the other two hands in Abhaya (protection) and Varada (giving boons) mudras. He has long matted hair from which flows the Ganga. He wears tiger and elephant skins, has necklaces of snakes and a garland of skulls and with a third eye in between the eyebrows. Parvati is his consort and Ganesh and Karthikeya are their sons. The Ganges shown flowing represents immortality.

The three eyes of Shiva represent the sun, moon and fire – the sources of light, heat and life. The third eye also indicates the eye of knowledge. With his third eye he sees the past, present and the future. When the eye of wisdom opens duality and forms get annihilated. He is known as Tryambaka as he has a third eye. The third eye is the eye of vision. It means a state of ultimate perception. Shiva Tattva is a no mind state of infinite consciousness.

A tiger kills its subjects and satisfies itself fully. It also represents lust. The wearing of the tiger skin represents mastery over desire. The elephant is a powerful animal and wearing its skin symbolizes destruction of animal impulses. It symbolizes control of pride.

The ash on his body indicates Him as the Lord of destruction. Ash is nirguna or devoid of properties and symbolises equanimity (vairagya) and reminds us of our mortal nature.

The garland of skulls represents the evolution and dissolution of generations of the human race that is the cycles of birth and death. They also represent that Shiva is beyond death.

His matted hair symbolises an ascetic. It symbolises the integration of the energy of our three bodies.

When the Kshirasamudra was being churned (Samudra Manthan) by the gods the crescent moon was rising and Shiva held it. He drank the Halahala (poison) to save the world. It was trapped and held in his throat which became blue in colour. He is therefore also called Neelankanta. The crescent moon stands for the mind and time. Thus he is one who has conquered the mind and is above time.

Shiva has his abode in Mount Kailash (celebration) in the Himalayas. He is handsome and snow white, white as camphor and that matches with his abode. White stands for the light that removes darkness and that one should be pure. Kailash means "Where there is only celebration". He is also said to be present in cremation grounds (nothing remains). He thus transcends duality. He is also shown in blue to signify immensity.

His meditative posture symbolises perfect harmony and bliss. His eyes are half open, half closed. It means that he is rooted in the Self or infinite consciousness while still active in the world. Shiva is calm, completely unaffected by his own energy and the process of the cycle of creation and destruction – in a state of satva (passivity) after annihilation of the gunas (qualities) tamas (dullness) and rajas (activity) i.e. victory over the body, mind, intellect complex symbolizing destruction of the ego.

Ganga represents purity and wisdom and therefore the one wearing it represents the power of purification. Ganges water stands for spiritual wisdom and hence a dip in the Ganges is considered sacred – symbolising union with the supreme. The Ganga flowing in trickles is the gradual spiritual development and the conveyance of spiritual truths to the people carefully and gradually. The trickling of the water of the Ganga symbolizes the flow of knowledge and immortality.

The trident indicates that he is the supreme ruler. It is a weapon of offence and defence. It represents creation, preservation and destruction. Also the three energy channels represented by the nadis in the spine i.e. Ida, Pingala, Sushumna. It also means among several other things the three gunas – sattva, rajas and tamas. Trishul represents three states of consciousness. Shiva is above these states and holding it means the divine is above these states. The trishul is a destroyer of all suffering.

His damaru (drum) produced the sounds of the Sanskrit language when he did the tandava. The damaru represents Sabda Brahman and the science of the language. It represents OM from which all the languages have come. The rosary indicates that he is the master of spiritual sciences.

The mirror indicates that the entire creation is a reflection of his self. The serpent represents ego with venomous desires. Man suffers due to victimization by his own desires. These can do no harm to Shiva, i.e. he is fearless, beyond death.

The serpent also represent wisdom, alertness and the individual jiva resting upon Shiva, the Paramatma. When an individual attains his Self he rests on Lord Shiva. The five hoods represent the five elements, and the five pranas. The snake is representative of the kundalini energy (Serpent Power).

The Bull is his vahana. It represents animal instincts and Shiva riding over it reflects his mastery. It is also a joyful bull of dharma having the four feet – truth, purity, kindness and charity.

He is also worshipped as the linga. The linga represents formless Brahman and infinity. Linga means mark or symbol in Sanskrit. It also means merge – the form into which all forms merge. Shiva tattva is formless. The Shiva linga is symbolic of the universe and its creator. It is symbolic of the Shiva and Shakti aspects of creation.

He is also worshipped as Dakshinamurti, the universal teacher, omnipresent and all knowing. He imparted knowledge to the first born sons of Brahma.

People pray to Him through the Panchakshri (five lettered mantra) Om Namaha Shivaya or the Mrityunjaya mantra among the several stotras. Shiva Sahasranama glorifies him (in his thousand names). His glories as the divine are sung in the Namaka and Chamaka sections of the Rudram. He is Mrityunjaya (conqueror of death) and devotees meditate on Him to avert calamities, accidents, illnesses and death. Shivaratri is the important festival of Shiva. Saints say that Om Namah Shivaya is a powerful mantra that helps uplift our consciousness.

Tandava is a dance representing the dissolution of the universe and in this form he is worshipped as Nataraja. The 108 modes of dances arose from Shiva. Shiva's dance (dynamism) indicates the continuous process of creation, preservation and destruction, the symbolic movement of the universe and the rhythm of Life. Tandava is the rigorous male aspect of dance of Shiva and Lasya represents the gentle female aspect of Parvati. The drum provides music to the dance of Shiva. It represents sound as the unfolding element of the universe. The raised left foot during the dance symbolizes release from rebirth along with the abhaya mudra meaning there is light ahead for a sincere devotee. Fire burns impurities. It purifies. The circle of fire (around Nataraja) represents reincarnation through endless cycles of births and deaths, the dance of nature emanating from Him and dissolving in Him. His foot is on a dwarf representing a man having covered himself from truth with ignorance and falsehood which prevents from realizing his essential nature. The Nataraja form represents the dance of creation created itself from eternal stillness.

Shiva pervades the whole world with his shakti. Uma represents prakriti, nature in her many perishable forms. Destruction can only associate itself with perishable matter.

He is Ashutosh or easy to please. He is also referred to as Mahadeva (the Supreme Lord), Maheshwara also means the same. He is Rudra the one who is strict and uncompromising, Neelakantha, the one with the blue throat, Chandrashekara, the Master of the moon and Shambhu (abode of joy), Dakshinamurti – south facing cosmic tutor, Kailashpati, the one who resides in Kailash, Umapati, the husband of Uma, Gangadhar the one who holds the Ganga, Pashupatinath, the Lord of all creatures. He is also called Mahayogi – the great ascetic symbolic of the highest form of penance and meditation. He is Sankara (Sam – happiness, Kara – giver), Sambasiva

(Sa – divinity, Amba – cosmos). He is also referred to as Panchanana (representing the five elements), Digambara, Bhuthanatha (Lord of all creation), Bhairava (the furious one), Bhuteshwara (Lord of elements), Yogeshwara (celestial ascetic), Mahakaala (Lord of time), Bhikshanatha (Lord of vegetation). Kalabhairava is a fierceful form of Shiva – when he destroyed time. All realities exist within a time span.

Shiva is fond of and is propitiated by Abhisheka. The greatest abhisheka is to pour the waters of pure love into the Lotus of your heart. Rudraksha - Rudra means Uncompromising and Aksha means eye. He is very strict with the operation of the cosmic laws. But with prayer he is known as an all 'giving' God, a lord of mercy.

Namaha means prostration. Namah Shivaya means prostration to Lord Shiva. Na is the screening power of the Lord that makes the soul to move in the world, Ma is the shakti that binds him in the samsara (the cycle of births and deaths), Si is the symbol of Lord Shiva, Va (his grace) and Ya (soul). Na represents Tirodhana (veiling), Ma (Mala or impurity), Si – Lord Shiva, Va (Arul shakti) and Ya (the soul).

In terms of the elements of the Universe Na stands for earth, Ma for water, Shi for fire, Va for air and Ya for space. These elements are also known as Sadyojaata, Vaamadeva, Aghora, Tatpurusha, Eesana. They represent four horizontal directions and the vertical respectively.

Ardhanareeshwara symbolises the two halves of creation comprising purusha and prakruti symbolising a need for balancing activity with dispassion and contemplation. Ardhanareeshwara does not mean half male and half female. It symbolizes the meeting of the male and female traits in an individual internally that can lead one to a state of ecstasy.

Shiva is known as Bholenath, because he is childlike. "Bholenath" means the innocent. He does not subject his intelligence to petty things.

Maha Shiva Ratri

Maha Shivaratri falls on krishna paksha chaturdashi night (14th night of the waning fortnight) of Maagha (in some calenders Phalguna). The monthly Maasa Shivaratri occurs each month on krishna paksha chaturdashi. Shivaratris are therefore twelve in a year. The one in Maagha is celebrated as Maha Shivaratri. It falls on a moonless night. Hindus offer special prayers to the lord of destruction. Maha Shivaratri means Great Auspicious Night (Shiva – Auspicious and Ratri – night). Darkness also symbolizes ignorance, the state in which most beings are in from a spiritual perspective. As this is a dark fortnight devotees light candles and lamps.

Of the many Hindu festivals only Shivaratri is celebrated in the night with an emphasis on prayers, meditation and inner journey. Ratri or night is that which gives comfort to the mind, body and soul and Shivratri is that which brings such a deep sense of serenity.

Meditation done on this day has a manifold effect. It astrologically links the Sun and the Moon in particular positions thus helping to elevate the mind. Maha Shivaratri marks the night when Shiva reveals Himself more easily and hence devotees observe fast or limited food to be able to receive the heightened energy especially at mid night which is beneficial for one's physical and spiritual well-being. During Shivaratri we take refuge in Shiva. As the upward surge of energy is high in the night on Shivratri many devotees try to keep awake at night.

Devotees chant Om Namah Shivaaya, a great mantra. The puranas explain the significance of this day.

Shiva means auspiciousness. The word ratri in Sanskrit means that which provides relief from of agony – ethereal, mental and material. Shivaratri literally means that night which infuses the Shiva tatva to the body, mind and speech.

Shivaratri marks the marriage day of Lord Shiva and Parvati. It is believed that Lord Shiva performed the cosmic dance of creation, preservation and destruction (tandava) on this day. Shiva manifested himself as a Linga on Shivaratri (you may refer to the Linga Purana) and is hence auspicious.

Shiva pervades in the entire universe. He has no form but is in every form. Shiva is one of the Trinity having control over destruction (Laya) or change as against Brahma for creation (Srishti) and Vishnu for sustenance (Stithi). "Laya" also means "Rhythm" leading to the concept of Nataraja. In addition to Srishti, Stithi and Laya, two less talked about acts are Tirodhana (Concealment) and Anugraha (Revelation). Tirodhana is the power of withdrawing creation at Maha Pralaya (Great Dissolution) while preserving essential elements of the universe and Anugraha is the reverse phenomenon i.e. to begin the creation. Laya, Tirodhana and Anugraha are performed by three aspects of Shiva – Rudra, Isvara and Sadashiva. Shiva is beauty, innocence and pure consciousness. Worshipping Shiva means to go deep within one's consciousness. Shiva is the lord of meditation, awakening (Shiva Tatva) and transformation.

Shivaratri is an occasion to awaken oneself from delusion. It is an opportunity to observe and recharge oneself on Shivaratri. Bilva leaves are offered to Lord Shiva, with fasting and being awake in the night. Our belief is that Goddess Lakshmi resides in the Bilva leaves and these are therefore considered sacred.

Kailash (Shiva's abode in Himalayas) means celebration. Wherever there is happiness Shiva is present. Shiva is a very simple and innocent and therefore known as bholenath. One just needs to offer bilva leaves to him. Bilva leaves signify the three tatvas of nature – Satva, Rajas and Tamas. One has to surrender the positive and negative aspects of one's life to Shiva. The best is to offer one's self to Shiva. Most people visit nearby Shiva temples and offer prayers although Shiva is everywhere.

Shiva is worshipped in many other forms each representing an aspect of his like Dakshinamurthy, Gangadhara, Maha Kaal, Nataraja, Shankara, Sambhu and so on. The thousand names (Sahasranama) of Shiva are given in Anusasanika Parva of Mahabharata, which also gives the sacred Hindu texts of Vishnu Sahasranama and Bhagavad Gita. Though Shiva is worshipped in many forms, he is not an incarnation deity like Vishnu.

Shiva Linga is a form in which Shiva is worshipped. There are different interpretations of Shiva Linga. The more profound meaning representing transformation between un-manifest and manifest. It represents the starting and ending of the creation. The Ellipsoid represents both Shiva and Shakti (Ardhanareeswara) with polarization commenced but not completed and is installed on a suitable circular base for worship with a cut in the periphery for collecting the Abhisheka Jal (water) and other ingredients. Abhisheka to cool the Shiva-Sakthi symbol is comparable to the cooling of the fission or fusion process for controlling energy release. Shiva Lingas are usually of stone (either carved or naturally existing shaped by the flowing rivers especially river Narmada). The Sri Rudram found in Yajurveda is chanted to pray to Shiva. The Shiva Mahimna Stotra and the Shiva Tandava Stotra are also sung with devotion.

Shiva when asked by Parvati replied that the 13th night of the new moon, during the Maagha month is the most auspicious. Once when all the worlds merged into Lord Shiva, in that darkness of nothingness Parvati worshipped Lord Shiva with great devotion. Shiva was pleased and blessed her. She requested Shiva for the benefit of all human beings that anyone who worships the Lord Shiva on this day with devotion should be blessed and given ultimate liberation. The generous Lord granted that thereby giving humanity the way to get blessed easily.

Tripundra is the three stripes of ash applied on the forehead by devotees of Lord Shiva. They are symbolic of spiritual knowledge, purity and penance (three eyes of Shiva). A rosary more famously known as mala, made of rudrakshas (these arose from the tears of Lord Shiva) is used by devotees worshipping Shiva. Water and bilva leaves are offered to the Linga. Other traditional practices include bathing the Linga in milk and Panchamrit (milk, curd, ghee, sugar and honey consecutively or smear it with kumkum or white consecrated rice (known as akshata – representing fertility) are also carried out worshipping the Lord.

There are twelve Jyotirlingas in India which are very sacred places and good for meditation. These are svayambhu lingas i.e they sprung up by themselves. The temples came up around them later.

There is a story in Shiv Mahapuran. Brahma and Vishnu had an argument on their superiority. Shiva appeared in the three worlds as an infinite pillar of light i.e the *Jyotirlinga*. Vishnu and Brahma tried to find the end of the light of the jyotirlinga in each direction Brahma came back from his search and lied that he gone up to and found the end, while Vishnu conceded defeat. Shiva then cursed Brahma that he would not be worshipped in ceremonies. Vishnu, however, would be worshipped until the end of eternity. The *Jyotirlinga* is the supreme reality from which Shiva appears. The temples which have the jyotirlingas are places where Shiva appeared as explained above. Each jyotirlinga takes the name of a different manifestation of Shiva. The primary idol in all the 12 temples is lingam representing the beginning-less and endless pillar, representing the infinite nature of Shiva. The jyotirlinga temples are ideal places for meditation. The twelve *jyotirlingas* are Somnath in Gujarat, Mallikarjuna at Srisailam (Andhra Pradesh), Mahakaleswar at Ujjain and Omkareshwar (Madhya Pradesh), Kedarnath (Himalayas), Bhimashankar (Maharashtra), Viswanath (Varanasi – Uttar Pradesh), Tryambakeshwar (near Nasik in Maharashtra, Vaidyanath at Jharkhand, Aundha Nagnath – Maharashtra), Rameshwar (Rameswaram – Tamil Nadu), Ghushmeshwar (Shiwar - Rajasthan), and Grishneshwar (Ellora/Aurangabad, Maharashtra).

People chant the Panchakshara Mantra, Om Namah Shivaya. The one who utters the Names of Shiva during Shivaratri, with greatest and heartfelt devotion is believed to be relieved from his sins.

The Shivapurana prescribes that one should fast and do Rudra Pooja. The Shivaratri Celebrations witness continuous chanting of Mahanyasa Purvaka ekadasa (11) rudrams for a period of 24 hours. Some temples have 11 such abhishekams during the period of 24 hours making it a total of 11 X 11 = 121 Rudrams.

As per the Puranas, a vessel full of poison emerged from the ocean during Samudra Manthan, The Gods and the demons were terrified as it could destroy the entire world. To protect the world he drank the poison and held it in his throat instead of taking it in. His throat turned blue and hence he is known "Neelakantha" (the one with a blue throat). Shivaratri is also celebrated as Shiva saved the world on this day. It is well known that Lord Shiva is abhishekapriya. Shiva is revered in his form for obtention of Jnana. Maha-Shivaratri is dedicated to the disintegration of the negativities of the Mind.

The Moon as well as the mind whose deity is the Moon have 16 phases. On Shivaratri there is just a streak of the Moon in the sky. The new Moon that follows will not have a visible streak. The mind too has to go through a similar transformation and only a trait remains to be removed through effort. That is the Sadhana that one does throughout the night on Shivaratri along with fasting and bhajans. When the mind dissolves there is no more desire and bondage leading one to moksha.

***

Shiva's family

Durga

DURGA

Prayerss to Durga / Divine Mother / Devi

**Sarva Mangala Maangalye Sive Sarvaartha Sadhike
Sharanye Tryambake Devi Narayani Namostute**

Prostrations to you, O Narayani. You bestow auspiciousness on all things auspicious. You give fulfilment in all fields of pursuits of all beings. You are merciful to all those who take refuge in you, O three eyed goddess, the consort of Shiva.

**Yaa Devi Sarva Bhuteshu
Matrurupena Sansthitaah
Yaa Devi Sarva Bhuteshu
Shaktirupena Sansthitaah
Yaa Devi Sarva Bhuteshu
Shantirupena Sansthitaah
Namastasyaih Namastasyaih
Namastasyaih Namo Namaha**

Oh Divine Mother, You are present everywhere and are the embodiment of the Universal Mother, of Energy and Peace, I bow to you.

**Chaturbhuje Chandra Kalaavathamse
Kuchonathe Kumkuma Raaga Shonc
Pundrekshu Pashamkusha Pushpabaana Haste
Namaste Jagadeka Mataa**

Oh Goddess with four arms, adorned with white garlands and pleasant face, Who has raised breasts and a face of the colour of kumkum, Who holds the bow of sugarcane, pasha, ankusa and flower arrows, My salutations to you Oh Mother of the universe.

Maanikya Veenamupalaalayanteem
Madaalasaam Manjula Vagvilaasaam
Maahendra Neeladhyuti Komalaangeem
Maatangakanyaam Manasaa Smaraami

Oh Goddess who plays the veena of emerald, Who is tired after great activity, Who has ability to speak sweetly and skillfully, Who is beautiful beyond comparison and is the daughter of Maatanga, I meditate on you.

Sri Annapoorna Ashtakam

Nityaanandakaree varaabhaya karee
soundarya ratnaa karee
nirdhootaakhila ghora paapani karee
pratyaksha maaheswaree
praleyaachala vamsa paavana karee
kasee puraadheeswari
bikshaam dehi krupaavalambana karee
maataannapoorneswari

Oh Mother Annapoorneswari, Who is The Goddess of Kasi, Who helps others with kindness, Who makes all days deliriously happy, Who gives boons and shelter to all, Who is the epitome of all beauty, Who cleans up all sorrows from life, Who is the ever-visible Goddess of the world, Who is the star of the family of Himavan, Please give me alms, Ocean of kindness and compassion.

Naanaaratna vichithra bhooshanakaree
hemaambaradambaree
muktahara vilamba maana vilasath
vakshoja kumbhaan tharee
kashmeera garu vaasithaa ruchi karee
kasee puraadheeswari
bikshaam dehi krupaavalambana karee
maataannapoorneswari

Oh Mother Annapoorneswari, Who is The Goddess of Kasi, Who is adorned with jewels of variety, Who is dressed in golden silk, Who has a beautiful chest, Adorned with golden chains full of gems, Who is the epitome of all beauty, Please give me alms, Ocean of kindness and compassion.

Yogananda karee ripukshaya karee
dharmaartha nishta karee
chandrarkaanala bhaasa maana laharee
trylokya rakshaa karee
sarvaishwarya karee tapah phala karee
kasee puraadheeswari
bikshaam dehi krupaavalambana karee
maataannapoorneswari

Oh Mother Annapoorneswari, Who is The Goddess of Kasi, Who gives bliss through Yoga, Who destroys enemies, Who makes dharma and wealth permanent, Who shines like moon, sun and fire, Who takes care of all the three worlds, Who gives all the wealth, Who fulfils all wishes, Please give me alms, Ocean of kindness and compassion.

Kailasaa chala kandaraalaya karee
gowri umaa sankaree
koumaree nigamaartha gochara karee
omkara beejaksharee
mokshadwara kavaata patana karee
kasee puraadheeswari
bikshaam dehi krupaavalambana karee
maataannapoorneswari

Oh Mother Annapoorneswari, Who is The Goddess of Kasi, Who lives in a cave in Mount Kailasa, Who is also called Gauri, Uma and Sankari, Who is an ever-blissful maiden, Who is known only through meaning of Vedas, Who is personification of "OM", Who opens the gates of Moksha, Please give me alms, Ocean of kindness and compassion.

Drishya drishya vibhooti vahana karee
brahmanda bandodharee
leela naataka soothra khelana karee
vijnana deepankaree
sri vishvesa manah prasadana karee
kasee puraadheeswari
bikshaam dehi krupaavalambana karee
maataannapoorneswari

Oh Mother Annapoorneswari, Who is The Goddess of Kasi, Who is the vehicle of the seen and unseen,

Who is carrying the universes inside her, Who cuts of attachment to this world, Who is the beacon of light for all science, Who makes the Lord of Universe happy, Please give me alms, Ocean of kindness and compassion.

Adik shaanta samastha varnana karee
shambo stri bhaavaa karee
kashmeeraa tripuresvaree trinayanee
visveswaree saarvaree
swargadwaara kavaata paatana karee
kasee puraadheeswari
bikshaam dehi krupaavalambana karee
maataannapoorneswari

Oh Mother Annapoorneswari, Who is The Goddess of Kasi, Who is described by all alphabets, Who gives Shambhu the three powers, Who is Kashmira the Goddess of three cities, Who is the intoxicant in three forms, Who gives rise to daily existence, Who is the enemy of all sorrows, Who fulfils the desire of every one, Who is dawn in life of all, Please give me alms, Ocean of kindness and compassion.

Urvee sarva janeshwari jaya karee
maata krupa saagaree
venee neela samaana kuntala dhari
nitya annadaaneswari
saakshanmoksha karee sadaa subha karee
kasee puraadheeswari
bikshaam dehi krupaavalambana karee
maataannapoorneswari

Oh Mother Annapoorneswari, Who is The Goddess of Kasi, Who is the Goddess of earth and its beings, Who is the knowledge, wealth and valour of the world, Who is the ocean of compassion, Who has lustrous blue hair, Who gives happiness to all, Who is personification of happiness, Please give me alms, Ocean of kindness and compassion.

Devi sarva vichitra ratna rachitaa
daakshaayanee sundaree
vaama swaadu payodhara priya karee
sowbhaagya maaheshwaree
bhaktaa beeshta karee sadhaa subha karee
kasee puraadheeswari
bikshaam dehi krupaavalambana karee
maataannapoorneswari

Oh Mother Annapoorneswari, Who is The Goddess of Kasi, Who is adorned with all precious gems, Who is the daughter of Daksha, Who is the epitome of beauty, Who feeds all the world her milk of song and writing, Who is the Goddess of all, Who is the fortune of all, Who fulfils the wishes of devotees, Who always does good, Please give me alms, Ocean of kindness and compassion.

Chandraarkaanala koti koti sadrushee
chandraamshu bimbhaadharee
chandraarkaagni samaana kuntala dharee
chandraarka varneswaree
maala pustaka paasankusa dharee
kasee puraadheeswari
bikshaam dehi krupaavalambana karee
maataannapoorneswari

Oh Mother Annapoorneswari, Who is The Goddess of Kasi, Who is like billions of moon, sun and fire, Whose smile is like the rays of the moon, Whose hair has the lustre of moon, sun and fire, Who is coloured like the moon and the sun, Who has a chain of beads and a book in her hands, Who has a spear and rope also in her hands, Please give me alms, Ocean of kindness and compassion.

Kshatra traana karee mahaa bhaya karee
maata krupa saagaree
sarvananda karee sadaa shiva karee
visveswari sreedhari
daksha krantha karee niraa maya karee
kasee puraadheeswari
bikshaam dehi krupaavalambana karee
maataannapoorneswari

Oh Mother Annapoorneswari, Who is the Goddess of Kasi, Who protects the duties of kings, Who gives great protection, Who is the great mother, Who is the ocean of mercy, Who gives perennial salvation, Who always does good, Who is the goddess of all universe, Who has all the wealth in the world, Who insulted Daksha, Who gives great health, Please give me alms, Ocean of kindness and compassion.

Annapoorne sada poorne
shankara praana vallabhe
jnana vyraagya sidhyartham
bikshaam dehi cha parvati

Oh Mother Annapoorneswari, Who is the darling of Sankara, Please give me alms, Of knowledge and renunciation, To me forever.

Maata cha parvati devi
pita devo maheshwarah
baandavaha shiva bakthaascha
swadesho bhuvana trayam

My mother is Goddess Parvati, My father is God Maheswara, My relations are the devotees of Shiva, And my country is the universe.

About Durga

Goddess Durga is the Shakti aspect of Lord Shiva. She is also known as Lalitha or Parvati. She is depicted in both peaceful and fearful forms. Durga (unapproachable or Goddess beyond reach – however, she is also a personification of tender love and affection).

Durga is the most widely worshipped as Shakti and Kali (Goddess of Destruction), ferocious and fearful forms. Durga appears when the evil forces become very strong.

All gods offer their power and radiance energise her form as Durga. 'Du' means evil, 'r' means diseases and 'ga' means destroyer. Durga or Kali has eight hands. She has an enormous power (shakti). Durga rides a lion.

As Kali she keeps her feet on the body of a demon. Kali comes from Kala – death or symbol of time. She is the goddess of time and transformation that is death. Kali is the kundalini shakti that keeps at bay the influences and attachments of the solar and lunar currents. People are afraid of death due to attachments. Kali creates fear in some and removes the fear of death in others. As Kali she is dark as the embodiment of tamas.

Parvati is known by other names as Girija, Himavati, Sarvani, Aparna, Uma etc. She is also known as Amba and Ambika or Divine Mother of the Universe. Kali is the first of the ten Mahavidyas i.e. the ten aspects of Shakti. They represent the transcendental knowledge, wisdom and power, the source of all knowledge. She is therefore known as Adya or first born. Bhairavi – consort of Bhairava (denies temptations of the world), Bhuvaneshwari (forces of the material world), Matangi, Kamala etc. As she had killed the demon Mahish she is known as Mahishasura mardini. She represents Prakriti.

As Parvati she is the daughter of the Himalayas (snow) and therefore Gowri (white). The Himalayas (Himavan) represents Aakasha or ether, the first fundamental substance. Mina her mother stands for intelligence. Parvati their daughter represents the conscious substance of the universe. She is Uma (bright one). On the spiritual plane she represents Brahma Vidya or spiritual knowledge and wisdom. Devi was formed out of the combined energy of the various gods.

Brahmi represents the primordial sound, the unmanifest sound, the word, OM. Vaishnavi is the power that gives the primordial energy a definite shape and order. Maheshwari is the power that gives individuality to the created beings. Karmani represents the ever present force of aspiration of the evolving soul. Varahi is the consuming power of assimilation and enjoyment. Indrani is the power that destroys any opposition to the cosmic law. Chamundi is the force of awakening that destroys the activities of the immature mind. She killed Chanda (fierce) and Munda (low) asuras to get the name Chamundi. Both are aspects of egoism in man. Shumba and Nishumba signify the higher aspects of our ego (Shumb means to shine).

She rides a lion, kills demons, with her several hands. The skulls and broken hands represent the state of destruction i.e. destruction of evil. Her hands represent the kinetic energy responsible for the dissolution of the created universe. The devotee invokes Durga to destroy desires, negative thoughts, false values and other such tendencies within himself.

There are various aspects of Parvati like Annapurna, Bala, Kameswari, Rajarajeswari, Bhadrakali, Katyayani, Vajreswari, Bhuvaneswari, Maheshwari etc. Like other Gods she is also seen in Abhaya and Varada mudras.

Navarathri

Ratri means night. Ratri gives rest to the body. Sound sleep energises the body and the mind. Ratri also means to take refuge. When the mind returns to the divine, there is real rest. Ra means night and tri means the three aspects of life. Nava means nine. So navaratri means giving rest to all the aspects of our life for nine days. Nav also means new. We should be new and regenerated after the nine days. During rest one is free of all the problems, conflicts, cravings that we have during our active state caused by the 5 sense organs and the action initiated consequently by the 5 karmendriyas or action organs.

The first three days are tamasic, the next three rajasic and the final three days satvic. We pray to Devi, our Divine Mother. She is a form of energy. She can destroy evil with the collective energy of Brahma, Vishnu and Shiva. Prayers during the Navaratri period or yagnas are meant for peace and prosperity not only for those who are praying but also for the entire humanity. They emanate vibrations that engulf the entire universe.

It takes nine days they say to go back to the source. During the first three days we pray to Durga or Kali, the ruling deity over the Tamas guna in us, the next 3 days we pray to Mahalakshmi (Rajas) and the final three days to Saraswati (Satva) to conquer our weak inherent tendencies, cravings, likes and dislikes. There is a significance to this order. It is subduing the lower nature (lower chakras) and proceeding further. First destroy the evil propensities in your mind, then implant divine qualities and finally Saraswati gives us true knowledge. Therefore action, contemplation and knowledge are the three stages through which we have to pierce through the veil of Maya, Prakriti or the three gunas.

Durga or Kali represents the destructive aspect of the divine within (Durga literally means unapproachable but she is very kind at heart), Lakshmi, the protective aspect and Saraswati, the knowledge aspect. Durga (Kriya shakti – the power of action), Lakshmi (Ichha shakti – the power of will) and Saraswati (Jnana Shakti – the power of knowledge). We purify ourselves and then direct our Ichha shakti to direct our mind to the divinity within. Ichha (left) and kriya (right) shakti are on either side whereas Jnana Shakti is in the middle.

Devi kills Mahishasura (the demon) who is symbolic of small mindedness. So Navaratri purifies our consciousness and consequently that of the entire universe. We form a new spirit and our samskaras or tendencies get erased, diluted and cleaned up.

The Devi killed the demons Madhu (Craving, Kama), Kaitabha (aversion, krodha), Shumba/Nishumba (doubt), Raktabijasura (tendencies not in our control), Mahishasura (dullness, tamas, inertia), Chanda (rebellious) and Munda (dullness) and Dhoomralochana (unclear perception). When these are destroyed Shakti, energy, purity, peace are established in us.

We all carry a beacon of light within us. When we go deep within ourselves and understand our Self, joy dwells in us. Mahishasura and Raktabijasura represent Vikshepa shakti – the tossing of the mind, the ever changing colour of the desires. Mala or dirt of the psychological structure of the mind (represents tamas) can be removed by Karma yoga and Vikshepa (represents rajas) by Upasana or worship.

The battle between Chamundeshwari and Mahishasura lasted nine days and nine nights.

The threefold transformation of the spiritual being of the devotee over nine nights brings in us – the power of the three presiding deities, that are manifested in us and help us in the upward ascent towards ultimate freedom. The aspiration of a human being is the soul's longing for freedom. Numbers are nine only. When you step over nine it is symbolic of eternity. There are nine planets. The body has nine openings. Bodily actions are ephemeral as the body only derives its value from spirit. Hence the body is a temple of God.

The tenth day is Vijayadasami which is celebrated as a victory day – to signify purification of oneself to conquer the evil forces. On the tenth day an effigy of Ravana is burnt to celebrate the victory of good (Rama) over evil (Ravana). It commemorates the victory of knowledge over ignorance. Rama worshipped Durga to fight Ravana to invoke her grace and power. Krishna also worshipped

Divine Mother. Arjuna deeply prayed to Devi before the battle of Mahabharata.

The tenth day is celebrated as Dassera. Dassera also stands for Dasa – Hara which means beheading the ten heads of Ravana. The ten heads represent hatred, jealousy pride, anger, greed, selfishness, infatuation, lust, passion, crookedness and ego. In a spiritual sense, navaratri epitomizes the stages of evolution of man from jivatma to paramatma.

***

Subrahmanya

Prayers to Subrahmanya

Om Shree Sharavanabhavaya Namaha

I prostrate to Lord Subrahmanya

Shadaananam Kumkuma Raktavarnam
Mahaamatim Divya Mayoora Vaahanam
Rudrasya Soonum Sura Sainya Naatham
Guham Sadaa Sharanamaham Prapadye

I seek refuge in the six faced God, the son of Rudra, who is the commander of the army of Gods, who has a vermilion complexion, who has supreme intelligence, moves on a divine peacock and always resided in the hearts of human beings.

About Subrahmanya

Subrahmanya is the second son of Shiva and Parvati after Ganesha. He is worshipped as very young and is known as the army chief of the gods or the celestial forces. He is also known as Kumara (young), Muruga (divineness or happiness in Tamil), Skanda (one who has the accumulated power of chastity), Karthikeya and Shanmukha. Subrahmanya means "one who tends the spiritual growth in devotees". He is born from the divine consciousness of Shiva.

Lord Krishna says in the Bhagavad Gita "Among the army generals I am Subrahmanya". He represents the great tapas (purification, penance) required of parents to have a son like him.

He is also known as Shanmukha – of six heads (also as Shadanana) which represent the five senses and the mind. The cumulative force of the five elements of the universe and the power of Shiva is Skanda. The six heads stand for the use of discriminative intellect is the six directions (four directions plus up/down) to overcome the six negative tendencies (Shad Vargas) i.e. Kama (desire), Krodha (Anger), Lobha (Greed), Moha (Infatuation), Mada (Pride) and Matsarya (Jealousy), that is, the qualities that impede spiritual progress. The six heads also represent the six attributes of wisdom, dispassion, fame, wealth and divine powers again indicating that he has the five senses and the mind under his control.

He explained the meaning of the Pranava or Om to his father in his role as a teacher and is hence known as Swaminatha.

He emerged out of the Sharavana (stands for reeds) lake when six Krittika maidens there emerged with six babies merging into single face. He was born in a forest with arrow like grass (Sharavana Bhava) and in the constellation Krittika (Karthikeya) with babies from six Krittika maidens.

He likes holy people (Brahmanas – who are immersed in Brahman) and is good to them (Su) and hence the name Subrahmanya. Su (beauty, goodness, joy) and Brahmanya (absolute knowledge). The state of turiya of restful alertness, which is beyond the states of waking, dreaming and sleep, is symbolized by Subrahmanya.

His weapon is the spear (lance or javelin) which stands for the shakti which provides knowledge and wisdom by eradicating ignorance and desires or vasanas. It shows one pointedness of the mind. The spear is an emblem of power.

His vehicle is the peacock which is shown holding a snake in one leg. Here the peacock represents the power of celibacy and the snake the lower instinctive desires in man.

The fully bloomed peacock represents the glory of creation of which he is the master. Thus it means that the power of celibacy can control lower desires and can take man towards spiritual development. The peacock is the enemy of the snake. The snake is not killed but held in captivity representing submission of the ego towards the higher Self within you. It also indicates fearlessness.

His consorts are Valli and Devasena representing the power of action (Kriya Shakti) and knowledge.

Subrahmanya Sashti is the day for the Lord. It is celebrated for six days preceding in the month of Margasira ending with Sashti. That is the day he defeated the demon Taarakaasura. The Skanda Purana is devoted to Lord Subrahmanya.

***

Hanuman

Prayers to Hanuman

Mano Javam Maaruta Tulya Vegam
Jitendriyam Buddhimataam Varishtam
Vaataatmajam Vaanara Yudha Mukhyam
Sriraama Dootam Sirasaannamami

I pray to the one who travels as fast as the mind and the wind, who has control over his senses, who is the most intelligent, who is the son of the wind God and the chief of the army of monkeys, who is the messenger of Rama, I bow down to you.

Hanuman Jayanti

Hanuman Jayanti is celebrated as the birthday of Hanuman who is widely worshipped in India. It is celebrated in Chaitra as per the Indian calendar. His birthday falls on Chaitra Shukla Purnima on a March/April full moon day. The Hanuman tattva (principle) is more active on this day of the year. Hanuman is an incarnation of Lord Siva. He was the son of the Wind-God (Vayu Devata) and Anjani Devi. He is also known as Pavanasuta, Marutsuta, Pavankumar, Bajrangabali and Mahavira.

Hanuman is worshipped for his unflinching devotion to Lord Rama. From early morning, devotees visit Hanuman temples to worship him. Hanuman is the symbol of devotion and strength. He can assume any form at will, wields rocks, can move a mountain in swiftness of flight. Of the five elements he represents the vayu (air) element without which there is no life. He had devotion, knowledge, selfless service and celibacy. He was never proud about his bravery. Hanuman is worshipped to overcome problems due to any negativity.

On this day (Chaitra Shukla Panchami), in a Hanuman temple spiritual discourses commence at dawn. Hanuman was born at sunrise. Discourses in temples are stopped and prasad is then distributed to those present. Discourses on spiritual texts are organised in most Hindu temples on this day. Parayan of Hanuman Chalisa on this auspicious day is very good to do.

Sindoor from Hanuman's body is applied on the forehead as tilak as this is believed to bring good luck. On an occasion when Sita was applying sindoor Hanuman asked her the reason. She replied that this would ensure a long life for Rama, her husband. Hanuman then applied sindoor all over his body to ensure Rama's immortality. Some devotees observe fast on Tuesdays and Saturdays. Hindus chant the name of Hanuman or the Hanuman Chalisa during difficult times. Many Hanuman Bhakts chant it daily. They also say "Bajrangbali Ki Jai".

Hindus believe that there are ten avatars of Vishnu. Each avatar comes with a specific purpose. Rama was Vishnu's avatar and had incarnated to destroy Ravana, the evil ruler of Lanka. To help Rama in his mission several gods accompanied him with their birth as well. Lord Brahma asked some gods and goddesses to be born as monkeys (known as Vanaras) to assist Rama. Indra was born as Vali, Surya as Sugriva; Brihaspati as Tara and Pavan was born as Hanuman, swiftest and strongest vanara.

Brihaspati had an aide Punjikasthala, who was cursed - who had to be born as a female monkey – this would only be redeemed if she gave birth to an incarnation of Lord Shiva. She was reborn as Anjana. She did a lot of tapas (penance) to please Lord Shiva, who then granted her a boon to release her from the curse. Lord Agni gave Dasharath, a bowl of dessert to share among the three of his wives to enable them to have divine children. However, an eagle took a portion of that desert and dropped it where Anjana was meditating. Pavan (God of Wind) delivered that into Anjana's hands who ate the dessert and gave birth to Hanuman.

Shiva was thus born as Hanuman to Anjana, with the blessings of Pavan who is indirectly also Hanuman's Godfather. Anjana was released from her curse with the birth of Hanuman. Anjana blessed Hanuman and told him that he would never die.

Anjana advised him that a fruit like the rising sun would be his food. Hanuman requested Surya to be his Guru and enlighten him on the scriptural knowledge. Surya agreed and that is how Hanuman became his disciple. Hanuman had to keep pace with his Guru while moving in the sky at equal pace, simultaneously taking his lessons. Hanuman mastered the scriptures in just sixty hours displaying extraordinary power of concentration.

Surya considered the speed of Hanuman's accomplishment as his guru dakshina. When Hanuman requested him to consider something more, Surya asked Hanuman to assist his son Sugriva as his minister.

Hanuman was always totally involved in the worship of Lord Rama. His extraordinary devotion made him free from physical fatigue. Hanuman is an example for all of us to utilise the power within us to awaken ourselves.

Hanuman is a great example of 'Dasyabhava' devotion – one that binds the master and the disciple. His greatness lied in his complete devotion to the Lord and an outstanding example of service to the Master.

While worshipping Hanuman, Sindoor is applied with the ring finger. Hanuman is worshipped to reduce the difficulties caused during the seven and half years astrological phase of planet Saturn.

The sacred thread on the left shoulder is symbolic of Brahmatej. He also had destructive powers as he was an incarnation of Shiva. However, due to his devotion to Lord Rama, the Vishnu-tatva also developed in him. In the Mahabharat when the Kauravas and Pandavas fought each other, Lord Krishna made Hanuman reside on flag of Arjuna's chariot. Hanuman protected Arjun by sometimes destroying the weapons before they could reach Arjun.

One of Shiva's eleven rudras was born as Hanuman. When Hanuman was young Surya gave him the knowledge of astras (weapons) and scriptures. He had felt that he should swallow the Sun which he saw as a red fruit. Indra hit him with his gada (thunderbolt) and prevented him in his endeavour. The Vajra (thunderbolt) hit his chin area – hanu, which became slanted and thus he is known as Hanuman. Indra, however, blessed him that he will never ever be defeated. Hanuman also obtained boons from Varuna dev (Rain God) and Yama – the God of death. Brahma gave him the power to overcome or to create fear. He was also granted the ability to travel anywhere at will.

Hanuman resolved problems with great devotion. He recited the glory of Raghu's lineage when hiding among the trees he saw Sita. This was done so that she would not misunderstand him to be one of the mayic forms of Ravan and gain trust. Overpowered by joy, she then asked Hanuman to present himself.

When Indrajit (Ravana's son) used miraculous weapons, Lakshmana became unconscious, Sushena, the physician asked them to get four types of herbs available on the Dronachal mountain for his revival. Hanuman displaying exemplary devotion flew and returned holding the mountain as he could not identify the herbs.

Sita gifted her pearl necklace to Hanuman during Rama's coronation. He broke a few pearls and had no interest in the necklace as he did not find Rama in them. When questioned about his devotion he tore open his chest to reveal that he had both Rama and Sita there to an audience in the palace assembly. Rama seeing his devotion embraced him and granted a boon. "Wherever people talk about me, you will always be there". Rama asked Hanuman "what can I give you?" Then he said "I will give you my love and grace and everlasting life". Your idol will also be there in any temple dedicated to me and you will also be worshipped.

Sage Valmiki said Buddhimataam Varishtham of Hanuman– the supreme among the wise, Jitendriya – one who has mastered his senses.

Hanuman served Sri Rama with great love and devotion, without expecting anything in return. He was an embodiment of humility and was completely unconscious of his great strength. Sri Rama asked Hanuman – how did you cross the ocean and burn Lanka? "By the glory of Thy Name, my Lord" replied Hanuman. He is therefore seen as a great karma yogi and a supreme devotee in total surrender.

As mentioned before Indra's thunderbolt hit Hanuman which not only wounded his chin but also made him fall and come down to the earth. Seeing him the wind-god himself was upset and did not visit the three worlds. The three lokas (worlds) were agitated (for want of air). Brahma and other gods went to calm down the wind-god. After calming down Indra, Hanuman's father carried him to Pathala. This endangered the all living beings due to lack of air. Brahma and the other gods went to Patala and pleaded with Pavan to return. To appease him they conferred boons on baby Hanuman. Brahma granted Hanuman a boon that he will be unconquerable and would never be defeated in combat.

Hanuman's life and his story is closely linked with that of Lord Rama and is covered at great length in Valimi's Ramayana and the Goswami Tulasidas's Ramacharitamanas.

Hanuman recognised his brother Bhima in the forest as both were born to Pavan. Hanuman pledged to help the Pandavas in the Kurukshetra battle. Hanuman kept himself on the flag of Arjuna's chariot and protecting it. The flag signifies control over the mind and senses and the prevailing of the higher nature over the lower nature.

Hanuman is said to be immortal (chiranjeevi). He inspires the sincere devotees of God. Tulsidas had the vision of the Rama due to the grace of Hanuman.

Rama asked Hanuman what attitude do you want towards Me? Hanuman answered: "Lord when I think I am the body, You are the Master and I am your servant, when I am jivatma, you are the paramatma and I am a part and when I am in supreme consciousness, we are both one - I see You as me and I as You."

***

Dattatreya

About Dattatreya

Dattatreya encompasses our Trimurti. Datta means selfless giving and Atreya comes from his father the Rishi Atri who was one of the Seven (Sapta) Rishis. Anasuya his mother was a Pativrata who served her husband with great devotion. She did severe penance as she wanted to have sons who will be equal to the Lords Brahma, Vishnu and Shiva in all respects.

There is a story about how sage Narada went about to fulfil this wish of Anasuya. The Trimurtis came to know about the desire of Anasuya. The Tri-Murtis came as Bhikshas and visited Anasuya as Sannyasis, asking her to bestow Nirvana. Anasuya was not clear what to do and she could also not decline their request. Sage Atri had gone for bath. She meditated on the form of sage Atri, surrendered to his feet and sprinkled over drops of water that was used for washing the sage's feet. The Tri-Murtis transformed themselves into three children due to the glory of the Charanamrit. Anasuya related what happened to Rishi Atri after the sage returned. The children were placed at his feet and worshipped him. Atri knew all about what had happened through his divine vision. With his embrace the three children transformed into one child with three heads and six hands. The Rishi blessed his wife. He then told her that the Tri-Murtis themselves were the children as they wanted to fulfill her wish. The three devis Saraswati, Lakshmi and Parvati who came to know of this through Narada appeared as ordinary women to the sage and asked for their husbands to be returned to them. The Rishi honoured the three ladies and prayed to them that both his wish and the desire of Anasuya should be fulfilled. The Tri-Murtis then appeared in their true form before the sage saying that the child will be equal to us. They gave him the name Dattatreya and blessed him.

Dattatreya left home at a young age in search of God. He attained enlightenment at Gangapure in Karnataka. Guru Gobind Singh said that Dattatreya was a Rudra avatar. Dattatreya's form varies as per the beliefs. The four dogs in various colours are representative of the knowledge of four Vedas: Dattatreya is considered to have come on earth as an avatar 16 times. Many consider Dattatreya to be their Adi Guru who appears in all yugas.

He propagated the philosophy of Avadhutopanishad and Jaabaaldarshanopanishad. His Avadhoota Gita was actually transcribed by two of his disciples. The *Dattatreya Upanishad* is part of Atharva Veda. He is the author of Tripura Rahasya, knowledge on Advaita that was given to Parasurama.

Srimad Bhagavat mentions about Dattatreya's discourse given to king Yadu in Treta Yug. There are references about him in the Ramayana and the Mahabharata. The Saandilya Upanishad mentions that Lord Dattatreya is the Supreme Reality.

He is worshipped in different ways in India. The Nath tradition consider Dattatreya as an Adi Guru and as an avatar of Shiva. He is worshipped on his birthday Datta Jayanti.

The first avatar of Dattatreya was Sripada Srivallabha who was from Pithapuram in Andhra Pradesh. There are various Datta Peethams in the country such as the one of Sri Ganapathi Sachchidananda Ashram in Mysore. The Datta peethams also worship Shakti, the Divine Mother. Dattatreya taught Parasurama, "Srividya" in order to enable him to get her grace.

Sage Atri and Anasuya are symbols of sacrifice and lack of jealousy. Dattatreya shows us that "giving" selflessly is the true sacrifice. Lord Dattatreya taught us to perform all our duties diligently and to the best of our ability. Yoga is the skill of giving up the sense of doership and the consequent desire to the fruits of our actions. It leads to eternal bliss that every one of us ultimately aspires.

***

Omkar Prayer

Omkaaram Bindusamyuktam
Nityam Dhyaayanti Yoginah
Kaamadam Mokshadam Chaiva
Omkaaraaya Namo Namaha

The yogis meditate on this syllable Om constantly which fulfils all our desires and brings about liberation. Salutations to Om again and again.

Morning Hymn

Karaagre Vasathe Lakshmi
Karamadhye Saraswati
Kara Muletu Govinda
Prabhate Karadarsanam

At the tip of my palms lives Goddess Lakshmi, in the middle Saraswati and at the base of the palm Govinda. This is how I look at my palms in the morning.

It is auspicious to look at your hand first thing in the morning.

Before Eating Food

Brahmaarpanam Brahma Havir
Brahmaagnau Brahmanaahutam
Brahmaivatena Gantavyam
Brahmakarma Samadhina.

Brahman is the ladle,
Brahman is the offering,
Brahman is the fire,
Brahman itself is the sacrifice

Brahman itself is the act of pouring the oblation into the fire, and Brahman is the goal which is reached by him who always sees Brahman in all actions.

For Health

Tejo si tejo mayi dhehi
Viryamasi viryam mayi dhehi
Balamasi balam mayi dhehi
Ojo si ojo mayi dhehi
Saho si saho mayi dhehi

O Lord do thou fill me with thy energy, Bestow strength on me, Grant power unto me, Inspire me with courage, do thou steel me with fortitude.

You can also repeat the Mrutyunjaya mantra.

Prayer for Good Intellect

Ya Ekoavarno Bahudhaa Shakti Yogaa
Dwarnaananekaan Nihitaatho Dadhaati
Vichaiti Chaante Vishwamaadu Sa Devah
Sa No Budhyaa Shubhayaa Samyunaktu

May the Divine Being, the one though Himself colourless, creates colours in different ways by means of His power, with a set purpose, and who dissolves the whole world in Himself in the end, endows us with a pure intellect.

Prayer for Success

Krishna Krishna Mahaayogin Bhaktaanaam Abhayankara
Govinda Paramaananda Sarvam Me Vashamaanaya

O Krishna, O Krishna, Thou art the Yogi of Yogis. Thou bestoweth fearlessness on Thy devotees. O Govinda, Thou art the giver of Supreme Bliss. Please bring everything into my favour.

Prayer for Prosperity

**Aayurdehi Dhanam Dehi Vidyaam Dehi Maheshwari
Samastha Makhilam Dehi Dehi Me Parameshwari**

Give me long life. Give me wealth. Give me knowledge, O Maheshwari. O Parameshwari, please give me everything that I desire.

Evening prayer when lighting the lamp

Shubham Karoti Kalyaanam
Arogyam Dhana Sampadah
Shatru Buddhi Vinaasaaya
Dipa Jyotir Namostute

I bow to the light of the lamp which brings brightness, auspiciousness, health, wealth all for the destruction of my bad thoughts.

Navagraha

Aadityaaya Somaaya Mangalaaya Budhaayacha
Guru Shukra Sanibhyascha Rahave Ketave Namaha

We take the names of all the navagrahas and prostrate
to them.

Sani

Neelaanjana samabhaasam ravi putram
yamaagrajam
chaaya maartaanda sambhuutam tam namaami
shanaischaram.

Mars or Kuja

Dharanee garbha sambhuutam vidyut kaanti
samaprabham
Kumaaram shakti hastam tam mangalam
pranamaamyaham.

Rahu

Ardh Kaayam mahaa veeryam chandraaditya
vimardanam
Simhikaa garbha sambhuutam tam rahum
pranamaamyaham.

Ketu

Phalaasa pushpa sankaasam taaraka graha
mastakam
Roudram roudratmakam ghoram tam ketum
paramaamyaham.

Hayagriva

Gnaanaanandamayam Devam
Nirmala Sphatikaakrutim
Aadhaaram Sarva Vidyaanam
Hayagriva Mupasmahe

I pray to Hayagriva, who is pure, like a white sphatika jewel and who is the lord of supreme education and bliss to bless us with knowledge.

Gayatri

Om Bhor Bhuvaha Swaha
Tat Savitur Varenyam
Bhargo Devasya Dheemahi
Dhiyo Yo Naha Prachodayaat

I meditate on the glory of God who has created the universe who is fit to be worshipped, who is pure knowledge and light, and who is the remover of all sins and ignorance. May he enlighten my intellect.

There are many other versions of the Gayatri for various Gods.

At night before sleep

Karacharanakrutam Vak Kayajam Karmajam Vaa
Shravana Nayanajam Vaa Maanasam Vaa
Aparaadham Vihitam Avihitam Vaa Sarvam Etat
Kshamasva
Jaya Jaya Karunaabdhe Shree Mahaadeva Shambho

Hail to thee Oh Lord Shiva, Lord of Lords, the ocean of compassion, please forgive the errors committed by me, knowingly and unknowingly, while performing actions with my feet, hands, speech, body, ears, eyes and the mind.

Rama Skandam Hanumantam

Vainatheyam Vrukodaram
Sayaneya Smare Nityam
Dusswapnam Tasya Nasyati

Oh Hanuman who has beautiful shoulders like the red
Ashoka tree, son of Vinatha with a stomach like that of
Vruka guard my sleep and keep bad dreams away and
grant me the privilege to think about you even during
my sleep.

Shanti Mantras

Om Bhadram No Apivataya Manaha
Om Shanti Shanti Shantih

Om. May my mind, the body, the senses, pranas may be good and well. Om Peace Peace Peace.

Om Bhadram Karnebhih Shrunuyama Devaha
Bhadram Pasyemaakshibhirya Jatrah
Sthirair Angais Tushtuvam Sastanoobhih
Vyashema Devahitam Yadaayuh
Swasti Na Indro Vriddhah Shravaah
Swasti Nah Poosha Vishwe Vedah
Swasti Nas Tarkshyo Arishta Nemih
Swasti No Brihaspatir Dhadhatu
Om Shanti Shanti Shantih

Om. O worshipful ones, may our ears hear what is auspicious. May we see what is auspicious. May we sing praise, live our allotted life span in good health and strength. May Indra who is extolled in the scriptures, Pushan the all knowing, Tarkshya, who saves us from harm and Brihaspati who protects our spiritual lustre, help us succeed in our study of the scriptures and the practice of the truths mentioned therein. Om peace, peace, peace.

Om Shan No Mitrah Shan Varunaha
Shan No Bhavatvaryaman
Shan No Indro Brihaspatih

Shan No Vishnuruurukramaha
Namo Brahmane Namaste Vayo
Twameva Pratyaksham Brahmaasi
Twameva Pratyaksham Brahma Vadishyaami
Ritam Vadishyaami Satyam Vadishyaami
Tan Maam Avatu Tadvaktaaram Avatu
Avatu Maam Avatu Vaktaaram
Om Shanti Shanti Shantih

Om. May the God of the day and the night, the God of strength, the God of intellect and the all pervading God be propitious to us. Prostrations to Brahman. Prostrations to thee O Vayu. Thou are indeed the visible Brahman. I shall proclaim thee the visible Brahman, the just and the true. May he protect me and the teacher. Om peace peace peace.

Mangalam Bhagavan Vishnuh
Mangalam Garuda Dhwaja
Mangalam Pundarikaaksha
Mangalayatano Harih

May auspiciousness be unto Lord Vishnu. May all auspiciousness be unto Garuda who rides upon the flagstaff of the Lord. May all auspiciousness be unto the Lord with lotus like eye. Lord Hari is the seat of all auspiciousness.

Om saha naavavatu sahanau bhunaktu
Saha veeryam karavaavahai
Tejasvi naavadheetamastu maa vidvishaavahai
Om shantih shantih shantih

May He protect us both (teacher and the taught)! May He cause us both to enjoy the bliss of Mukti (liberation)! May we both exert to discover the true meaning of the sacred scriptures! May our studies be fruitful! May we never quarrel with each other! Let there be threefold peace.

Namaste sate te jagat kaaranaaya
Namaste chite sarva lokaashrayaaya
Namo dvaita tattwaaya mukti pradaaya
Namo brahmane vyaapine shaashvataaya

Salutations to that Being, the cause of the universe! Salutations to that Consciousness, the support of all the worlds! Salutations to that One Truth without a second, which gives liberation! Salutations to that pure, eternal Brahman who pervades all regions!

Om yaschandasaamrishabho vishwaroopah
Chhandobhyo dhyamritaat sambabhoova
Sa mendro medhayaa sprinotu
Amritasya devadhaarano bhooyaasam
Shareeram me vicharshanam
Jihwaa me madhumattamaa
Karnaabhyaam bhoori vishruvam
Brahmanah Koshoasi medhayaapihitah
Shrutam me gopaaya
Om shantih shantih shantih!

May He, the Lord of all, pre-eminent among the Vedas and superior to the nectar contained in them, bless me with wisdom! May I be adorned with the knowledge of Brahman that leads to immortality! May my body

become strong and vigorous (to practise meditation)!
May my tongue always utter delightful words! May I hear
much with my ears! Thou art the scabbard of Brahman
hidden by worldly taints (not revealed by impure, puny
intellects). May I never forget all that I have learnt! Om
peace, peace, peace!

Om aham vrikshasya rerivaa
Keertih prishtham gireriva
Urdhwapavitro vaajineeva swamritamasmi
Dravinam savarchasam
Sumedhaa amritokshitah
Iti trishankor vedaanu vachanam
Om shantih, shantih, shantih!

I am the destroyer of the tree (of samsar; worldly life). My
reputation is as high as the top of the hill. I am in essence
as pure as the sun. I am the highest treasure. I am all-
wise, immortal and indestructible. This is Trishanku's
realisation. Om peace, peace, peace!

Om aapyaayantu mamaangaani vaak
Praanashchakshuh shrotramatho
Balamindriyaani cha sarvaani sarvam
brahmopanishadam
Maaham brahma niraakuryaam maa maa brahma
niraakarod
Niraakaranamastva niraakaranam me astu
Tadaatmani nirate ya upanishatsu dharmaaste
Mayi santu te mayi santu.
Om shantih, shantih, shantih!

May my limbs, speech, Prana, eye, ear and power of all my senses grow vigorous! All is the pure Brahman of the Upanishads. May I never deny that Brahman! May that Brahman never desert me! Let that relationship endure. Let the virtues recited in the Upanishads be rooted in me. May they repose in me! Om peace, peace, peace!

Om vaang me manasi pratishthitaa
Mano me vaachi pratishthitam
Aaveeraaveerma edhi vedasya ma aanisthah
Shrutam me maa prahaaseer anenaadheetena
Ahoraatraan samdadhaami ritam vadishyaami
Satyam vadishyaami tanmaamavatu
tadvaktaaramavatu
Avatu maam avatu vaktaaram avatu vaktaaram
Om shantih, shantih, shantih!

Let my speech be rooted in my mind. Let my mind be rooted in my speech. Let Brahman (Supreme Reality) reveal Himself to me. Let my mind and speech enable me to grasp the truths of the Vedas. Let not what I have heard forsake me. Let me spend both day and night continuously in study. I think truth, I speak the truth. May that Truth protect me! May that Truth protect the teacher! Let peace prevail against heavenly, worldly and demoniacal troubles. Om peace, peace, peace!

Om yo brahmaanam vidadhaati poorvam
Yo vai vedaanshcha prahinoti tasmai
Tam ha devmaatma buddhi prakaasham
Mumukshurvai sharanamaham prapadye

Om shantih, shantih, shantih!

He who creates this entire universe in the beginning, and He about whom the Vedas gloriously praise and sing, in Him I take refuge with the firm faith and belief that my intellect may shine with Self-knowledge. Om peace, peace, peace!

Om vishwaani deva savitar duritaani paraasuva
Yad bhadram tanma aasuva

O all pervading, Supreme Lord, the effulgent Creator, we place our faith and trust entirely in Thee. Keep away from us all that is evil and bestow upon us all that is good.

Om agne naya supathaa raaye asmaan
Vishwaani deva vayunaani vidvaan;
Yuyodhyas majjuhu raanmeno
Bhooyishthaam te nama-uktim vidhema.

O Supreme Lord, who art light and wisdom, Thou knowest all our thoughts and deeds. Lead us by the right path to the fulfilment of life, and keep us away from all sin and evil. We offer unto Thee, O Lord, our praise and salutation.

Tvamekam sharanyam tvamekam varenyam
Tvamekam jagatpaalakam svaprakaasham;
Tvamekam jagatkartu paatruprahartru
Tvamekam param nishchalam nirvikalpam.

O Thou my only refuge, O Thou my one desire, O Thou the one protector of the world, the radiant One. O Thou the creator, sustainer and dissolver of the whole world, O Thou the one great motionless Being, free from change and modification.

Vayam tvaam smaraamo vayam tvaam bhajaamo
Vayam tvaam jagat saakshiroopam namaamah;
Sadekam nidhaanam niraalambameesham
Bhavaambhodhi potam sharanyam vrajaamah.

O Thou eternal all-pervading witness of the whole universe, we meditate on the one Truth. We silently adore Thee and offer Thee our salutation. We take complete refuge in that one Almighty Being, the basis of everything, self-supporting and supreme, a vessel in the stormy sea of life.

Om dyauh shaantih Antariksham shaantih
Prithivee shaantih Aapah shaantih
Oshadhayah shaantih Vanaspatayah shaantih
Vishvedevaah shaantih Brahma shaantih
Sarvam shaantih Shaantireva shaantih
Saamaa shaantiredhih
Om shaantih, shaantih, shaantih!

First interpretation:

O Supreme Lord, Thy celestial regions are full of peace and harmony; peace reigns on Thy earth and Thy waters. Thy herbs and trees are full of peace. All Thy forces of nature are full of peace and harmony. There is peace and perfection in Thy eternal knowledge; everything in the universe is peaceful, and peace pervades everywhere. O Lord, may that peace come to me!

Second interpretation:

May peace radiate there in the whole sky as well as in the vast ethereal space everywhere. May peace reign all over this earth, in water and in all herbs, trees and creepers. May peace flow over the whole universe. May peace be in the Supreme Being Brahman. And may there always exist in all peace and peace alone. Om peace, peace and peace to us and all beings!

Concluding Prayers

Namastwanantaya Sahasra Murtaye
Sahasra Pada Akshi Shiroru Bahave
Sahasra Namne Purushaya Shashvate
Sahasra Koti Yuga Dharine Namaha

Salutations to the eternal Purusha who has innumerable names and forms, feet, eyes, heads and hands who is eternal and ageless. Salutations again to the infinite divine reality.

Kayena Vahcha Manaseindriyairva
Budhyatmana Va Prakrute Svabhavat
Karomi Yadyat Sakalam Parasmai
Narayanayeti Samarpayami

I offer unto the supreme Lord Narayana whatever I do with my body, speech, mind, sense organs, intellect, from my whole being.

Om Sarvesham Svastir Bhavatu
Sarvesham Shantir Bhavatu
Sarvesham Purnam Bhavatu
Sarvesham Mangalam Bhavatu
Sarve Bhavantu Sukhinah
Sarvesantu Niramayah
Sarve Bhadrani Pashyantu
Ma Kaschit Dukha Bhaag Bhavet
Lokaah Samastaah Sukhino Bhavantu

May all be blessed, May all be peaceful, May all be fulfilled, May auspiciousness prevail.

May all be cheerful and happy, May all be free from illness, May all see auspiciousness, May none ever be unhappy.

Om Asato Ma Sad Gamaya
Tamaso Ma Jyotir Gamaya
Mrityorma Amritam Gamaya

Lead me from untruth to truth
From darkness to light, and
From death to immortality

Om Purnamadhah Purnamidham Purnaath
Purnamudhachyate
Purnasya Purnamaadaya Purnamevava Shishyate

Om. That (universal soul) is infinite. This (individual soul) is infinite. From the infinite becomes manifest as the infinite. From the infinite when the infinite is negated what remains is the infinite. Om Peace, peace, peace.

Sarve Janaaha Sukhino Bhavantu

May All People Be Happy.

Four attitudes to have

(refer Patanjali Sutras)

Maitri Friendliness, Pleasantness
Karuna Compassion
Mudita Goodwill
Upeksha Acceptance, Neutrality and Equanimity

Four Stages of Life

Our life has four stages. The first phase is Brahmacharya where knowledge is important. Brahma represents the first phase, Saraswati providing the knowledge. The second phase is Grihasta (householder). As we reach adulthood and get married our responsibilities increase and we fulfil our worldly, social, and family duties through our activity represented by Vishnu for which wealth is required (Lakshmi). Vanaprastha is the third stage where one starts to get detached and works for the pursuit of knowledge (Shiva and Shakti). All these fall away in the fourth stage (Sanyasa) through renunciation and deep meditation.

Bhagavaan – God, Supreme Soul, Universal Spirit

Bha Bhoomi, Earth element. The earth totally accepts what anyone does.

Ga Agni, Fire. Purifies, prepares, destroys.
Va Vayu, Air. Like the mind travels fast.
A Akash, Space. Limitless. Provides for everything to exist.
N Neer, Water. Adaptable, Seeks the deepest level.

Essentially, the Pancha Mahabhutas or the Five elements of which the Universe is made.

Why 108 beads in the Rosary or Mala?

There are many reasons why 108 – I give here only a few.

a. 9 planets multiplied by 12 constellations = 108

b. 9 planets by 12 houses

c. There are 108 marmas or energy intersections in the subtle body. There are said to be totally 108 energy lines converging into the heart chakra

d. The Sanskrit alphabet has 54 letters – each with masculine and feminine aspect equalling totally 108.

e. The diameter of the Sun is 108 times the diameter of the earth. The distance of the Sun to the Earth is 108 times the diameter of the Sun. The average distance of the Moon from the Earth is 108 times the diameter of the Moon.

f. Man breaths 21,600 breaths a day of which half are solar energy and half are lunar energy i.e. 10,800. That is 108 multiplied by 100.

g. There are 108 dance forms of Shiva.

There are many other reasons as well not covered here.

Chanting

I am giving a few quotations here about the importance of chanting.

Value of Chanting – Excerpt from the book "Bhajans" by Sri Sri Ravi Shankar

Sounds are particles of infinite energy. Definite sounds create definite patterns of energy. So, in singing, the words, the sounds, they create that energy in your system – in your nervous system. They purify, alleviate and energize the nervous system. Something starts happening. Very profound, very deep, very beautiful.

Glory of the Name – From Japa Yoga by Swami Sivananda

Just as fire has the natural property of burning inflammable things, so also the Name of God has the power of burning sins, samskaras and vasanas and bestowing eternal bliss and everlasting peace on those who repeat it.

Sri Ramakrishna Paramahansa – extracts from his quotations

Japa means repeating the name of the Lord silently, sitting in a quiet place.

If you chant the name of God clapping your hands at the same time, the birds of evil thoughts will fly away from the tree of your body.

Pray to God in any way you like. He is always sure to hear you. He can even hear the footfall of an ant.

Pray with a sincere and simple heart and your prayers will be answered.

A.C.Bhaktivedanta Swami Prabhupada

To chant the names of God is very purifying and it will lift one from the material platform to the spiritual. The easiest way to be fixed in constant association with God is through chanting His names.

Prayer Materials and their Significance

Tilak – A mark of auspiciousness. If applied at the space between the eyebrows it has a cooling effect. Sandal paste has a spiritual influence. It reduces the heating effect when you concentrate at this point. The material used may be ash (for Shiva devotees), Kumkum is sacred to all Gods particularly for Devi and Devi devotees) and sandal paste for Lord Vishnu. It enables attention on the Ajna chakra and lifts energy upward and helps in retaining energy within the body.

Achamana – Sipping water three times before eating while repeating the Lord's name. The sprinkling of water around the plate while chanting mantras purifies the food.

Pictures, Idols – These are forms that help concentration. Image worship makes it easier and it also denotes that God is present everywhere including in objects like the pictures, idols etc.,

Bells – The use of bells shuts out external sounds to enable the mind to concentrate.

Aarti/Waving of Lights – Denotes that the Lord is all self effulgent light. We pray "Remove the darkness in me and bestow your divine light. May my intellect be illumined"

Incense Sticks – The fragrance spreads throughout the prayer room and denotes that the Lord is all pervading. Let our desires and impressions vanish like the smoke of the incense.

Camphor – Denotes that the individual ego should melt like camphor and the individual should become one with Supreme Light.

Sandal Paste – Reminds a devotee that he should be, in his difficulties, as patient as Sandal. Sandal gives fragrance only when crushed into a paste. We should be cheerful and happy even when crushed like Sandal.

Prasad – Sacred offering to the Lord. Lord Krishna says in the Bhagavad Gita "whoever offers a leaf, flower, fruit or even water with devotion, that I accept, offered with a loving heart."

Tarpan – Offering of water to the gods

All the above may be outward symbols and not an end in themselves but they do help in concentration.

Temples

Temples are places with high energy. The main idol is placed in the centre (the sanctum sanctorum or known as garbhagriha) under the idol where the energy is high and a copper plate inscribed with some Vedic scripts is buried beneath the main idol in the "Garbhagriha" which has the impact of radiating energy in the areas around the temple. Idol worship helps focus and concentration during prayer

A person who visits a temple and makes clockwise pradakshina receives the emitted magnetic waves which get absorbed by his body. The Garbhagriha is completely enclosed on three sides. The energies is very high inside the sanctum sanctorum. A temple is a place to charge one's own body battery. As a temple is a consecrated place in the past there used to be temples particularly in South India every couple of lanes away so that people can live within the consecrated space of a temple. The ringing of the bells removes distractions enabling the mind to be focussed on devotion to the God in the temple.

The lamps in the temple radiate the heat and light energy. The ringing of the bells and the chanting of prayers generates sound energy. The fragrance of the flowers, the burning of camphor give out energy as well. All these energies are activated by the positive energy that comes out of the idol in the sanctum sanctorum. The water used for the pooja is mixed with Cardamom, Benzoine, Tulsi, Clove, etc. is called "theertham". This water becomes more energized because it receives the positiveness of all these energies combined.

When persons go to the temple for Deepaaraadhana or an arti ceremony and when the doors open up, the positive energy gushes out from the sanctum sanctorum onto the people waiting for the darshan of the God in the form of the idol. The water when sprinkled onto the people passes on the energy to all. That is the reason men are asked not to wear shirts to the temple and ladies have to wear ornaments because it is through these jewels that positive energy is absorbed in ladies.

Theertham (usually three spoons taken one after the other) is a good blood purifier as it is highly energized. This water is a source of magneto therapy as they place the copper water vessel at the Garbhagriha. Cardamom, clove and saffron add taste to the Teertham and Tulsi leaves in the water increase its medicinal properties. The clove essence protects one from tooth decay, the saffron & tulasi leaves essence protects one from common cold and cough, cardamom and benzoine (as Pachha Karpuram) serve as a mouth refreshener.

The peepal tree has the property of absorbing and releasing large quantities of oxygen even in the night.

The Tulsi has medicinal properties. Lord Vishnu is fond of this plant. In view of this it is also planted in homes.

Mango Leaves

We all find that the Indian homes decorate the main door of the house with a garland (thoranam) of mango leaves. This is also true of areas where rituals are performed. The real reason for this tradition needs to be understood. There is a scientific meaning behind the hanging of the leaves. Fresh green mango leaves are pleasing to the eye and the mind. Green leaves absorb carbon dioxide and release oxygen. Thus the surroundings are kept hygienic with more oxygen.

The air is thus purified when it passes through the leaves. Various insects also move towards the garland thus keeping the people in the house safe. Being around in greenery calms the mind and lowers anxiety. Even yellow leaves after falling from the tree continue photosynthesis for sometime. They last longer than other leaves.

It is common to use dry mango leaves to treat certain ailments. The dry mango leaves powered, mixed with coconut oil are used in first aid for cuts and wounds.

Mango leaves we are told to absorb the negative energy from anyone entering your home or a place where a ceremony is being performed.

It is believed from ancient Pauranic times that the mango tree is personified by various Gods and is a symbol of fertility.

Mango leaves are also placed in the Kalasam with a coconut.

It is also common practice to apply turmeric paste on the door of a house as it has anti-septic and anti-bacterial properties. Turmeric applied around the door stops bacteria and other microscopic organisms from entering the house.

Some of our customs

Namsakar: I bow down to the divinity in you. The joining of the fingers helps activate the nerve endings or pressure points there which have a corresponding centre in the sense organs. It is a healthy way of respecting the person without physical contact.

Touching the feet of elders: Blessings flow into the younger person from the elderly and wise who are at peace through their hands and toes.

Fasting: Fasting helps the body to cleanse itself of toxins. It is good for health.

Things to Know

Ten Avatars of Vishnu

Matysa (Fish)
Koorma (Tortoise)
Varaha (Boar)
Narasimha (Man-Lion)
Vamana (Dwarf)
Parasurama
Rama
Krishna
Buddha
Kalki (yet to come)

Seven Rishis

As per Brahmana:

Vashista,
Bharadvaja,
Jamadagni,
Gautama,
Atri,
Visvamitra, and Agastya,

As per the Brihadaranyaka Upanisad:

Gautama,
Bharadvāja,
Viśvāmitra,

Jamadagni,
Vashiṣṭa,
Kaśyapa,
Atri, and
Brighu

Four Vedas

Rig Veda
Yajur Veda
Sama Veda
Atharva Veda

The Rig Veds has Sanskrit hyms praising God and also prayers.

The Yajur veda – Shukla Yajurveda and Krishna Yajurveda have mantras to inspire and perform good actions.

The Sama Veda has slokas uttered in musical form. The sound waves generated from various slokas can provide mental peace etc.

The Atharva Veda covers yoga, physiology, social and other issues. Ayurveda is a part of this Veda

Six Vedangas

These are considered as the limbs of the Vedas. They are:

1) Shiksha (phonetics, Pronunciation of words)
2) Kalpa (ritual)
3) Vyakarana (grammar)
4) Nirukta (etymology)
5) Chandas (meter)
6) Jyotisha (astronomy – also covers astrological aspects)

Six Philosophies

There are six schools of thought which accept the Vedas as supreme authority. These are:

1) Samkhya – a dualist theory consciousness and matter.
2) Yoga – which covers meditation, contemplation and liberation.
3) Nyaya or logic – which explore the sources of knowledge through Nyāya Sūtras.
4) Vaisheshika – an anti-mysticist school of orthopraxy
5) Vedanta – highest knowledge in the Vedas
6) Mimamsa – Pursues freedom through action, duty.and rituals

Three Vedantic schools

The three Vedantic schools are Advaita (non duality propagated by Shankaracharya), Vishishtadvaita (Qualified Monism by Sri Ramanujacharya) and Dvaita (duality – Sri Madhavacharya).

Three Gunas

The three gunas are our tendencies and are referred to as sattva, rajas, and tamas. Sattva represents the qualities of goodness and purity. Rajas represents of drive, ambition, and passion. Tamas represents darkness, laziness and lack of sensitivity.

Four Mahavakyas

There are four Mahavakyas from the four Vedas. These Vakyas from the Upanishads indicate the unity of the Jivatma (Individual Soul) with Paramatma:

Aham Brahmasmi (I am Brahman)

Tat Twam Asi (Thou art That)

Ayamatma Brahma (This soul is God)

Pragnanam Brahma (Consciousness is Brahman)

There are other **mahavakyas** as well which are:

Brahma satyam jagan mithya (Brahman is the truth; the world is unreal)

Ekam evadvitiyam brahma (Brahman is one, without a second)

Soham (He I am)

Sarvam khalvidam brahma (Everything is Brahman)

Four Yogas

Gnana Yoga – The Path of Knowledge
Bhakti Yoga – The Path of devotion
Karma Yoga – The Path of action
Raja Yoga - Meditation, Kriya, Pranayama etc

Seven Lokas

The seven lokas are Bhur (Earth), Bhuvah (the world of air with astral beings, Suva (Swarga with the Devas such as Indra etc.), Maharloka (the abode of radiant beings), Janaloka (the abode of deities), Tapaloka (that of pure souls) and Satyaloka (Truth).

These are above the earth but there are several patalas or lower regions in the universe located below the Earth.

Sahasranamas

These are the 1008 names of a deity.

There are many Sahasranamams and these include Vishnu Sahasranamam, Lalitha Sahasranamam, Lakshmi Sahasranamam, Ganesha Sahasranamam, Shiva Sahasranamam, Durga Saharanamam, Subrahmanya Sahasranamam. Vishnu and Lalitha Sahasranamas are more popular.

Four Yugas

1) Sat Yuga
2) Treta Yuga
3) Dwapara Yuga
4) Kali Yuga

The Hindu Months

The 12 months of the Hindu Calendar starting with Chaitra usually in the third week of March are:

1) Chaitra
2) Vaisakha
3) Jyaistha
4) Ashadha
5) Shravana
6) Bhadrapada
7) Asvina

8) Kartika
9) Agrahayana
10) Pausa or Pushya or Dhanurmas
11) Magha
12) Phalguna

The Hindu Moon Days

The 15 Moon Days of the Hindu Month starting with Prathama are:

1) Prathamā or Pratipada
2) Dvitïyā
3) Trtïyā
4) Chaturthï
5) Pañchamï
6) Sasthï
7) Saptamï
8) Astamï
9) Navamï
10) Dasamï
11) Ekādasï
12) Dvadasï
13) Trayodasï
14) Chaturdasï
15) Panchadasï
16) Purnimā – Full Moon
17) Amāvāsyā – New Moon

Vibhuti (Sacred Ash)

The vibhuti reminds us about the mortal nature of our life. It is a medium to transfer energy and helps in the control of the subtle body. It can be made from cow dung and also rice husk. The body is just like the husk of a rice grain. Sacred ash if prepared properly and applied at some points makes a person more receptive to higher energies. Yogis usually wear ash received from the cremation grounds. Vibhuti is generally applied between the eyebrows, where the agna chakra is located. It can also be applied at the throat and the heart areas where there are other chakras in the subtle body. If your energies are strong they can influence your surroundings. There is a science behind this, and in our culture properly prepared sacred ash has a different vibrancy.

Nine ways of devotion

The sages have said that there are nine ways to express devotion to God. They are:

1) Sravanam (listening to God's glories),
2) Keerthanam (singing the glories of God),
3) Vishnusmaranam (ever remembering the Lord),
4) Paadasevanam (worshipping the Lord's feet),
5) Archanam (offering daily worship),
6) Vandanam (prostration),
7) Daasyam (dedicated service),
8) Sneham (friendliness), and
9) Atmanivedanam (total surrender).

History has shown that people have practised one of these methods some of whom became great saints.

The Five Bhavas

A Bhava is an attitude that one can adopt in one's relationship towards the divine. These are essentially found among the bhaktas. These are shanta bhava, dasya bhava, sakhya bhava, vatsalya bhava and madhurya bhava.

Shanta Bhava – A devotee in shanta bhava endeavours to develop peace and experiences God as supreme peace. A good example of this type of bhava is Bhishma, the grandsire or pitamaha of Mahabharat.

Dasya Bhava – The attitude of a sevak or servant of God. The bhakta feels humble and as a servant of the Almighty God. Hanuman is a good example in this category in his relation to Rama.

Sakhya Bhava – The devotee considers the Almighty as his dearest friend, a very intimate relationship. Our religion permits this kind of relationship with the Divine. Arjuna's relationship towards Krishna is described as one of friendship and an example for this bhava.

Vatsalya Bhava – is the attitude of Motherly Love. The devotee cultivates a feeling of motherly affection towards God. Vatsalya is an intimate relationship and natural for most women. Yashoda, the foster mother of Krishna loved Krishna as if he was her own child.

Madhurya Bhava – the bhakta sees God as his beloved lover. It is most intimate among the bhavas. It is one of the high forms of devotion. The relationship between Radha and Krishna is an example of this type of bhava. Mirabai and Chaitanya Mahaprabhu are other examples.

Through any one of the above bhavas, the mind gets cleansed and one's antahkarana gets purified.

12 Jyotir Lingas

There are 12 jyotirlingas in the country (India). These are:

a) Somnath in Guajarat
b) Mallikarjunswamy in Srisailam (Andhra Pradesh)
c) Mahakaleshwar in Ujjain, Madhya Pradesh
d) Omkareshwar in Madhya Pradesh
e) Viadyanath in Maharshatra
f) Nageshwar in Maharashtra
g) Kedarnath in Uttaranchal
h) Tryambakeshwar in Nasik, Maharashtra
i) Rameshwaram in Tamil Nadu
j) Bhimashankar in Maharashtra
k) Vishweshar in Varanasi, Uttar Pradesh
l) Grishneshwar in Maharshtra

It is believed that by the darshan of these jyotirlingas we get blessed and the darshan brings about happiness in our lives.

There is a sloka repetition of which helps us to remember the 12 jyotirlingas.

There are other famous Shiva Lingas – Kanchipuram, Tiruvannamalai, Chidamabaram and Jambukeswaram in Tamil Nadu and Sri Kalahasti in Andhra Pradesh.

Purnima

Purnima or Pournami is a full moon day. For Hindus each full moon day has special significance. The masters who are in other planes are said to descend on to the earth and bless the people. There is an upsurge of energy and if one meditates the energy goes up the spine and works for the devotees benefit. It is known that the moon has an impact on the tides. Similarly, as water constitutes a large part of a human body, a person is also affected by the moon. It is very good to do *full moon meditation* on this day. It is good to fast on the full moon day. Satyanarayan Puja vrata can be performed as well on all full moon days

The 12 Purnimas

The list of poornimas are given as per the months January to December although as per the Hindu Calendar Chaitra is the first month which coincides with March/April.

Shakambhari Purnima or Paush Poornima in the month of Pausha or Pushya (January)

Magha Poornima (February) – Parvati is worhsipped on this day. Prayers are also offered to Brihaspati.

Phalgun Purnima – Holi, the Spring Festival of Colours occurs in this month (March).

Hanuman Jayanti in the month of Chaitra (April). Some states celebrate it on different dates.

Vaisakha Poornima (May) – Also known as Buddha Poornima – the day of enlightenment of Lord Buddha. Also his birthday.

Jyestha or Vat Purnima in the month of Jyeshta (June). Women pray for their husbands by tying threads around a banyan tree (Vat) on this day. It honors Savitri, the legendary wife of Satyavan who escaped death for her husband's life. It is the chosen day for worshipping Yama deva.

Guru Purnima – devotees worship their Guru in Ashada Maas (July). This is also Vyasa Purnima. Sage Vyasa is considered as the Guru of all. The Guru principle is at its highest this month. This is the day for gratitude to one's Guru.

Sharad Purnima – the Autumn Harvest Festival, on a full moon day. It is said that Krishna and the gopis performed the Raas Leela on this day.

Shravan Poornima (August) – Hayagriva Jayanti is also celebrated on Shravana Purnima, also known as Nariyal

Purnima. Raksha Bandhan is celebrated on this day. It is also important for performance of "Upanayanams". It is considered as an important month for worship to Lord Shiva. Rudra poojas are organized in this month.

Madhu or Bhadrapada Purnima in the month of Bhaadrapada (September) – Devotees perform Uma Maheshwara Vrata. Lord Indra is worshiped for children. Satyanarayana is worshipped on this day.

Ashwin Poornima – Goddess Lakshmi is worshipped in Ashwin (October).

Kartika Poornima – in the month of Karthika (November). The demon Tripurasura was defeated by Shiva. Subrahmanya and Vishnu are also worshipped on this day. However, this month people usually pray to Lord Shiva. Rudra poojas are organized.

Dattatreya Jayanti in the month of Margashira (December) – Lord Krishna is worshipped on this day.

The months mentioned above are indicative and sometimes a poornima could come in an earlier month, for example.

Vaikuntha Ekadasi

Vaikuntha Ekadasi is a sacred day and is in Margasira or Dhanur Maas i.e in December/January. Ekadashi is the

11th day of the lunar fortnight and is observed mainly in the temples of Lord Vishnu.

Fasting is observed on this day and is considered very auspicious as stated in the Vishnu Puran. Those who cannot fast may take fruits and milk. Namasankirtan is organised by some on the day. The thus purified mind develops devotion and gratitude.

The churning of the ocean (Samudra Manthan) took place on this day. Amrit (nectar) emerged out of the ocean and was given to the devas. It is believed that those who die on this day are freed from the rounds of birth and death.

In the *Srimad Bhagavad Gita,* Krishna says among the months I am Marghasira. Nammalwar, a saint in the lineage of Sri Ramanuja went to Vaikuntha on this day and was received by Lord Vishnu. It was also on this day that Lord Krishna gave the Gita discourse to Arjuna on the battlefield of Kurukshetra. It is on this day that the doors of Vaikuntha are opened. The Vishnu Sahasra Nama was revealed to Bhishma on this day.

It is revealed in the Padma Purana, the female energy of Vishnu killed Muran, a demon (symbolic of lust, passion, inertia, arrogance) as the devas were being harassed by the demon. Vishnu needed a new weapon to kill him as it was proving difficult otherwise. To create a new weapon, Vishnu took rest in a cave in Bhadrikashrama named after the goddess Haimavati. Muran tried to kill the sleeping Vishnu and then, the feminine power from

Vishnu emerged to burn down Muran to ashes with just a glance. A pleased Vishnu named the goddess Ekadashi and granted her a boon that those people who fast on this day should go to Vaikunth.

Generally rice is not eaten on this day (there is also a story not covered here) as it could be heavy and hamper the night vigil. Heightened awareness helps a person overcome his negative tendencies.

Akshaya Tritiya

Akshaya means that which does not diminish. It is in the month of Vaisakh (April/May). Both the Sun and the Moon are in exalted positions on that day, and this happens only once in a year. It is also known as Akha Teej in some parts of India. It is a day for wealth acquisition; the Lakshmi tatva is high for both material and spiritual activities. The festival is also celebrated by the Jain community. A bath in the Ganges, fasting and charity are good things to do on this day. Important things about this day are:

This is a day for Lord Vishnu.

It is the birthday of Parasuram, an incarnation of Vishnu.

Krishna presented an Akshaya Patra to the Pandavas, a bowl which could produce an endless supply of food for the needy.

Veda Vyasa commenced writing of the Mahabharat on this day.

It is believed that Ganges descended on the earth this day.

The Treta Yug started on this day.

It is good day to start new ventures and construction of property.

Goddess Annapoorna was born on this day.

Krishna provided protection to Draupadi on this day in the palace when the Kauravas were insulting her.

Adi Shankara sang the Kanakadhara Stotram in the house of a poor family which he had visited for alms.

It is also an occasion for weddings.

Kubera, the Lord of wealth, himself prayed to Goddess Lakshmi on this day.

Goddess Chamundeshwari killed a demon on this day.

Krishna's poor friend Sudama visited him on this day and as he had nothing much to offer, he took poha to offer to Krishna. On Sudama's return to his hut he found that it had been converted into a palace.

In most of the years, even banks in India sell gold coins.

Raksha Bandhan Chants

Sister's chant to a brother(s) on Raksha Bandhan in North India:

"Suraj shakhan chhodian...meaning Mooli chhodia beej Behen ne rakhi bandhi, Bhai tu chir jug jee"

"Yena baddho Balee raajaa daanavendro mahaabalah, tena twaam anubadhnaami rakshe maa chala maa chala"

Symbols

In Hinduism we use a lot of symbols. Each symbol has a specific meaning.

Wheel the cycle of time.

Trident symbolic of the three states of consciousness, three gunas and creation, preservation and destruction.

Lotus purity. It lies in dirty water but is still pure.

Conch shell sound of ocean waves that brings liberation. Represents the sound OM.

Ganga purity. Pure stream of knowledge.

Blue complexion infinite consciousness.

Swan power of discrimination as it can separate milk from water.

Moon tranquillity of the mind.

Flute hollow and empty – one who has transcended his self.

Lion immense strength. vehicle of Durga

Trunk used by elephant for smell as well as an organ of action. Symbolises dual consciousness.

Snakes represent alertness. Also tamed passions.

Mala helps in chanting and centres the mind.

Four (or many arms) supreme power.

Tiger skin symbolizes a mind lost in the web of desires.

Book knowledge.

Sweets refined state of consciousness.

Axe remover of obstacles – it was the first instrument invented by man.

Sword the power to destroy fear & ignorance.

Raised right palm an assurance of protection.

There are many other such symbols such as club, arrow, mace and also musical instruments, animals (e.g. rats, elephants, peacock etc.) which have different meanings.

Mantras

Mananat Trayate Iti Mantraha

(That by the constant thinking of which one gets protected is a mantra)

There are scores of mantras.

The more well known ones are:

Gayatri mantra (Vishwamitra was the seer or rishi of this mantra)

Om Nama Shivaya (known as Panchakshri)

Om Namo Narayanaya (known as Ashtakshri)

Om Namo Bhagavate Vasudevaya

Hare Rama Hare Rama, Rama Rama Hare Hare, Hare Krishna Hare Krishna, Krishna Krishna Hare Hare (known as Maha mantra)

Om Gum Ganapathaye Namaha

Om Dum Durge Namaha

Sri Rama Jaya Rama Jaya Jaya Rama

Hari Om and many others

Many devotees repeat just the God's name such as Shri Rama, Shiva, Krishna or Vithal Vithal etc. with Bhakti.

A Saguna mantra has a seer and a presiding deity. It has a meter and a seed sound which has power. Every mantra has Shakti. By constant repetition of the mantra its chaitanya is awakened.

***

Gayatri

The Gayatri Mantra

Scientific aspects

Continous chanting of this mantra generate powerful vibrations that could induce divine effects by vibrating all subtle glands, nerves, neuronal passages and extrasensory energy centres in the physical, subtle and astral bodies. Chanting of Gayatri Mantra stimulates emission of supernormal brain impulses.

The sound waves that are created, when Gayatri Mantra is said, is of the shape of a ring. It rises up with great speed, through the medium of ether and goes towards Sun, and after touching the surface of the Sun, it returns back along with the powers of Sun such as heat, radiance, light and other powers which are very subtle. The stronger the faith, concentration and will attached with the Mantra, the higher the benefit.

Views

Theosophist scholar Mr. Leadbeater attributes distinctive significance to the collective chanting of Gayatri Mantra in his book "Man – Visible, Invisible". The sonic waves along with the sublime currents of Sabd Shakti produced by the chanting of the mantra propagate upwards in a spiral shape and expand up to the heart of Sun (the deity of Gayatri Mantra). The echo of these is reflected back and bestows the supernatural energy and flow of prana and divine brilliance of Sun on the body, mind and inner self of the chanter.

Arthur Koestler, a renowned thinker, philosopher in an interview to "Blitz" magazine said commenting on nuclear wars - "The great Gayatri Mantra is more powerful than thousands of atom bombs. If all of India collectively chants this mantra, the power aroused thereby would annul all hazards of nuclear warfare and protect the globe...".

"The Best Divine Prayer Hymn in the World!" - Dr. Howard Steingeril, an American scientist, collected Mantras, Hymns and invocations from all over the world and tested their strength in his Physiology Laboratory. He concluded that the Gayatri Mantra is the most rewarding scientifically. That the Gayatri Mantra produced 110,000 sound waves per second. This was the highest and found it to be the most powerful prayer hymn in the world - *Source: daily.bhaskar.com.* Also found in many other websites. It is understood that a German university initiated this research into the efficacy of the Gayatri Mantra.

***

Om Shanti

Om Shanti is usually chanted thrice after a prayer. This is done to give us inner peace, peace in the world, and peace in the soul. One can also interpret this as peace in body, speech, and mind, or as a wish for peace individually, collectively and universally.

Kalasha

A Kalasha is a pot of brass, copper or an earthen pot. Mango leaves are kept in the opening with a coconut covering the mouth of the pots which are sometimes decorated – these represent creation. White thread (or red thread) is tied around the pot in a diamond shape pattern. The threads symbolises the love that binds all. The pot is filled with water (sometimes with rice). The water is symbolic of the primordial water from which the creation emerged springing from the energy behind the universe. It represents a lifeless body filled with divine life force which helps us perform our various activities. It is called Purnakumbha.

A kalasha which symbolizes auspiciousness is kept for important rituals at home such as house warming, poojas and weddings. The saints are full of happiness, love and respectfulness and hence it is kept at the entrance to welcome saints with a purnakumbha as a mark of respect for them.

Lord Vishnu was reclining on his snake-bed in the milky ocean prior to creation. Brahma appeared in a lotus which emerged from Vishnu's navel and then started creation. During the churning of the milky ocean, the Lord appeared holding the pot of nectar and blessed one with everlasting life and hence a kalasha is also a symbol of immortality.

The blessings of all the deities are invoked into the kalasha and its water is thereafter used for all the rituals. A temple's consecration is done with rituals including the pouring of one or more kalashas of holy water on the top of the temple.

Slokas corroborated by science

There are many things scientific in our religion. We do not know the reason for many practices and hence consider them as tradition or superstition. For example:

Everyone knows the Hanuman chalisa? In Hanuman Chalisa, it is said:

Yug sahastra yojan par Bhanu!
Leelyo taahi madhur phal janu!!

1 Yug = 12,000 years
1 Sahastra = 1,000
1 Yojan = 8 Miles

Yug x Sahastra x Yojan = par Bhanu
12,000 x 1,000 x 8 miles = 96,000,000 miles

1 mile = 1.6 kms

96,000,000 miles = 96,000,000 x 1.6 kms

= 1,536,000,000 kms to the Sun

NASA has said that, it is the exact distance between Earth and Sun (Bhanu). This proves that Hanuman ji did know of the distance from Earth till Sun, when he was thinking it as a sweet fruit (Madhur phal). It is really interesting how accurate and meaningful our ancient scriptures are. Unfortunately, it is barely recognized, interpreted accurately or realized by anyone in today's time.

Sanskrit

The slokas are in Sanskrit, the most ancient language. Sir William Jones had declared "The Sanskrit language, whatever be its antiquity, is of a wonderful structure: more perfect than the Greek; more copius than Latin and more exquisitely refined than either."

He who knows my grammar knows God said Panini, the great Indian Philologist paying tribute to the mathematical and psychological perfection in Sanskrit. (Source – Autobiography of a Yogi).

Peepal Tree

This is a tree that produces large amounts of oxygen even at night. In the Bhagavad Gita, Krishna said "Among the trees I am the Ashvattha tree". There is reference to the peepal tree as being a symbol of Vishnu (refer Skanda Puran). It has medicinal properties. Buddha obtained his enlightenment under the Ashvattha tree also known as Bodhi tree.

Tulsi

Has medicinal properties and is believed to improve immunity.

Two Pakshas

Krishna Paksha
Shukla Paksha

Three Runas (Debts)

Dev
Pitru
Rishi

Four Shankara Mutts

Dwaraka
Sringeri
Joshimath
Jagannath Puri

Panchagavya

Ghee
Dudh
Dahi
Gomutra
Gobur

Five Elements

Earth
Water
Fire
Air
Space

Meanings

Om	Primordial sound, the word, an expression of the Supreme Brahman.
Vishnu	That which pervades everywhere.
Rama	One who is radiant within (Ra-radiant and Ma-myself).
Vasudeva	In-dweller, All Pervading Intelligence.
Paramatma	Supreme Self.
Krishna	Most attractive, Dark one (Krish – to be, Na – final emancipation).
Maya	Delusion.
Govinda	One who is known through the declarations of the scriptures. There are other meanings as well.
Shiva	Transcendence, Bliss, The Auspicious Self.
Japa	Repetition of a Mantra or God's name.
Bhajan	Sharing. Sharing all that is divine.
Bhakti	Surrender (Bha – fulfilment, Ka – knowing, Ta – salvation, I – energy).
Shraddha	Faith, dedication.
Satsang	Company of the wise who know the Truth.
Atman	Self.
Diksha	Initiation (Di – Intellect, and Ksha - Horizon or End).
Vedanta	Highest knowledge.
Dhyayeth	I meditate.
Namaskar	I bow down to the divinity in you.

Bija	Seed word. Many mantras have seed words. Gum is the seed word for Ganesha, Aim for Saraswati etc.
Abhyasa	Practice
Acharya	Teacher
Adhyatmic	Spiritual
Ahamkara	Ego
Ajnana	Ignorance
Ananda	Bliss
Ananta	Endless
Archana	Offering at the time of worship
Artha	Wealth
Avatara	Incarnation of God
Bala	Strength
Brahma	Creator
Brahman	The Absolute
Bija	Seed sounds
Buddhi	Intellect
Chaitanya	Pure Consciousness
Darsana	Vision
Dhyana	Meditation
Devata	Deity
Daya	Compassion
Devi	Goddess
Deha	Body
Gada	Mace
Ishwara	Lord, God
Jnana	Knowledge
Karuna	Compassion
Karma	Action, Cause & effect
Kirtan	Devotional songs

Maharishi	Great Sage
Mahatma	Great Soul
Manas	Mind
Matsarya	Jealousy
Mauna	Silence
Moha	Attachment, Infatuation
Mukti	Liberation
Muni	Saint
Murti	Idol, Picture
Nadi	Nerve
Nidra	Sleep
Nitya	Eternal
Padma	Lotus
Prana	Life force
Purusha	Divine Being
Samsara	Worldly life
Samskara	Impression
Shanti	Peace
Satya	Truth
Sutra	Aphorism
Tapas	Austerity
Vasanas	Subtle desires
Vaikuntha	Abode of Lord Vishnu
Vak	Speech
Narayana	Supporter of the souls. Ayana – support, ra – perishable, na – not.
Purushottama	Supreme Individual Soul.
Madhusudhana	One who is sweet like honey, killer of the demon Madhu.
Keshava	One who has lovely locks of hair. Also killer of Keshi.

Janardhana	Who destroys the wicked, protects us from the wicked.
Hrishikesha	The Lord of the senses.
Madhava	Consort of Universal Mother, Ma Lakshmi, attained Madhu Vidya, Lord of everyone.
Giridhari	One who held/lifted the Govardhana Mountain.
Govinda	Go – Cow, Senses, Earth, Vinda - one who pleases. One who is praised by the Gods, who confers the Vedas and protects the Cows.
Vishwakarma	Celestial Architect
Kamala	Nayan One with lotus eyes
Gopal	Protector of Knowledge
Srimad	Beautiful
Sankara	The giver of happiness. Sam – Blissful/ Awareness/Happiness and Kara – the giver, the one who causes it.
Linga	The formless into which all forms merge.
Ishwara	The Supreme Being. Ish – to control, Wara – person i.e. controller
Lokas	Worlds
Tarpan	Offering water to the Gods, ancestors' souls and human beings and satisfying them through this action is called tarpan.
Sloka	A prayerful verse
Guru	Gu – Darkness, Ignorance, Ru- Dispeller
OM	Symbol of God

Bhuh	Bhu Loka
Bhuvah	Astral Plane
Swaha	Celestial Plane
Tat	That, Paramatman
Savitur	Ishwara
Varenyam	Fit to be worshipped
Bhargo	Remover of sins and ignorance
Devasya	Shining
Dhimahi	We meditate
Dhiyo	Intellect
Naha	Our
Prachodayat	Enlighten, Guide
Swami	One with the Self i.e. immersed in truth/God
Sanyasi	comes from Samyasyati. Sam means together, ni means down and asyati means to throw. One who throws down his identity and no relation to relatives, objects, countries, etc. There is no longer a sense of mine.

Please note that some words have more than one meaning which is not included here.

Ten types of Shuddhis (Purifications)

Body gets purified by water and exercise
Breath gets purified by pranayama
Mind gets purified by sense control
Intellect gets purified by knowledge
Memory gets purified by meditation
Ego gets purified by seva (service)
Self gets purified by silence (maun)
Food gets purified by positive thoughts while cooking
and eating
Wealth gets purified by giving
Bhav (inner feelings) gets purified by love

Bhakti

When bhakti enters food, it becomes Prasad
When bhakti enters hunger, it becomes a fast
When bhakti enters water, it becomes charanmrith
When bhakti enters travel, it becomes a pilgrimage
When bhakti enters music, it becomes kirtan
When bhakti enters a house, it becomes a temple
When bhakti enters actions, it becomes services
When bhakti enters in work, it becomes karma, and
When bhakti enters a man, he becomes human

This page has been reproduced with the consent of
Tumuluru Krishna Murty

ADI SHANKARACHARYA

This book is a compilation of
the important Hindu prayers, Gods and festivals
of all time. It is meant for anyone who wishes
to have a basic introduction to Hinduism. These
prayers and festivals in honour of Hindu Gods are the
path set by our sages and ancestors. Understanding
and following this path will lead one to knowledge
about our culture and the symbolism in
Hinduism.

Hayagriva Stotram

Gnananandamayam devam nirmala sphatikakrutim,
aadharam sarvavidyanaam Hayagreeva mupasmahe.

I worship Lord Hayagreeva, who is the very form of
knowledge, pure as a crystal, and who is the support of
all knowledge.

Dakshinamurthy Stotram

Om Namah Pranavaarthaaya Shuddha Jnyaanaika
Murtaye
Nirmalaaya Prashaantaaya Dakshinaamurtaye Namah
Salutations to the embodiment of Pranava (Om),
Salutations to the personification of the Pure Knowledge,
Salutations to the Pure and unblemished, Salutations to
the Tranquil,
Salutations to Sri Dakshinamurthy.

Nidhaye Sarva Vidyanaam Bhishaje Bhava Roginnaam
Gurave Sarva Lokaanaam Dakshinamurtaye Namah

Salutations to Sri Dakshinamurthy
Who is a receptacle to all Knowledge,
Who is a healer of all the diseases of Worldly bondage,
Who is a Guru to all the Worlds,
Salutations to Sri Dakshinamurthy.

Suggested Readings

1. Japa Yoga - Swami Sivananda, Divine Life Society, 1992
2. Hindu Gods and Goddesses - Swami Harshananda, Ramakrishna Math, 1981
3. An Intimate Note to the Sincere Seeker - Sri Sri Ravishankar, Sri Sri Publications Trust, 2010
4. The Symbolism of Hindu Gods and Rituals - A.Parthasarathy, Vedanta Life Institute, 1983
5. Talk on Krishna by Sri Sri Ravishankar
6. Prayer book, Ramakrishna Centre, South Africa, 2001
7. Lord Siva and His Worship - Swami Sivananda, Divine Life Society, 1992
8. Website www.dlshq.org
9. In Indian Culture, why do we - Swamini Vimalananda, Central Chinmaya Mission Trust